"All that we have done,
you have done for us."
ISAIAH 26:12 NRSV

"No one can come to me
unless drawn by the Father who sent me."
JOHN 6:44 NRSV

"By grace you have been saved through faith,
and this is not your own doing;
it is the gift of God."
EPHESIANS 2:8 NRSV

"God does not guide me,
he pushes me forward, he carries me away,
I am not master of myself."
MARTIN LUTHER

"Only God himself
can let the bucket down to the depths in us."
C. S. LEWIS

Other Books by Robert K. Hudnut

Emerson's Aesthetic
Meeting God in the Darkness
This People, This Parish
The Bootstrap Fallacy: What the Self-Help Books Don't Tell You
Church Growth Is Not the Point
Arousing the Sleeping Giant: How to Organize Your Church for Action
The Sleeping Giant: Arousing Church Power in America
A Thinking Man and the Christ
A Sensitive Man and the Christ
An Active Man and the Christ
Surprised by God: What It Means to Be a Minister in Middle-Class America Today

CALL WAITING

HOW TO HEAR GOD SPEAK

Robert K. Hudnut

InterVarsity Press
Downers Grove, Illinois

InterVarsity Press
P.O. Box 1400, Downers Grove, IL 60515
World Wide Web: www.ivpress.com
E-mail: mail@ivpress.com

InterVarsity Press® is the book-publishing division of InterVarsity Christian Fellowship/USA®, a student movement active on campus at hundreds of universities, colleges and schools of nursing in the United States of America, and a member movement of the International Fellowship of Evangelical Students. For information about local and regional activities, write Public Relations Dept., InterVarsity Christian Fellowship/USA, 6400 Schroeder Rd., P.O. Box 7895, Madison, WI 53707-7895.

Cover photograph: Tony Stone Images

ISBN 0-8308-2213-5

Printed in the United States of America ∞

Library of Congress Cataloging-in-Publication Data

Hudnut, Robert K.
    Call waiting : how to hear God speak / Robert K. Hudnut.
      p.   cm.
    Includes bibliographical references.
    ISBN 0-8308-2213-5 (pbk. : alk. paper)
    1. Vocation—Christianity.   2. Vocation—Biblical teaching.
    I. Title.
    BV4740.H83   1999
    248.4—dc21   99-34680
                                                                                                            CIP

21 20 19 18 17 16 15 14 13 12 11 10 9 8 7 6 5 4 3 2 1

16 15 14 13 12 11 10 09 08 07 06 05 04 03 02 01 00 99

For Mary

Foreword

Here speak the voice and the heart of a pastor. Bob Hudnut has lived caringly and attentively as a pastor for a long time. All that time he has noticed a great deal. And now he mobilizes what he has noticed in order to mediate a world of deep spirituality that is not clever or cloying or coercive.

This voice and heart are *deeply attentive*. Hudnut notices in acute ways what people say and how they feel and how they manage and how they decide. He is able to take the most ordinary happening and turn it enough to make it luminous.

This voice and heart have the *accents of wisdom*. Hudnut finds pithy ways to make us stop and reconfigure what we thought was fully cased out. The book teems with things to remember which we wish we had said.

This voice and heart are *saturated with biblical content and imagery*, done quickly, poignantly so that the Bible "connects." Abraham is called in the everyday circumstances of his life. Moses is "in the wrong job" when he is called. Singing Mary is credited with beginning an economic revolution.

The voice and heart speaking here *have access to the lore of our spiritual-intellectual inheritance*, so that Hudnut lets us into his library and into his file of "best quotes." In addition to Irenaeus and Augustine, there are Dante and Kierkegaard, Carlyle, Wesley, Hopkins, Zorba and even Chuck Colson. The treatment is breezy. Hudnut does not linger to find out if we agree or even understand. Before we get to vote, he is off to the next page and the next topic with a dozen other insights that will carry us beyond where we have been.

All of this vast, informed, imaginative sensitivity is not exhibitionism, and it is not self-indulgence. Hudnut is occupied with a serious, urgent agenda. He is aware that our "outer lives" are so driven and full and pressed that we end up deeply numbed. He joins the struggle for a life of faith in a culture that is organized against serious faith, a culture which invites a self-preoccupation and emptiness that lead to brutality toward self and neighbor. Hudnut offers a powerful antidote to emptiness, and so takes us to the hunger that belongs to our true selves, a hunger almost evaporated in the junk food all around.

But this book is not another book of spirituality or psychology. Hudnut knows and cares about genuine spirituality, but he also knows about self-indulgence and narcissism. He knows about psychology and is not inimical to it, even though he can do a stunning piece on dreams without any Jungian ideology.

What matters is that here speaks *a grounded, gentle Calvinist* who understands that faith is not self-satisfaction, but it is referencing one's life to God, a recentering of self that drives one to issues of justice and mercy. The incessant focus of this wondrous statement is not friendly assurance or solace, but it is in *call*. It is being addressed by God's holiness in ways that dislocate and relocate.

The happy focus of this book about call, moreover, is in an *incarnational* orientation. The notion of "listening points" is Hudnut's way of identifying the occasions, locations and circumstances wherein God may call and we may answer toward God's newness. The substance of the book is the assertion that everywhere, every time, in any circumstance is a potential listening point for those who have ears to hear. And even when we lack appropriate ears to hear, we are often addressed in ways that give us ears we did not want in order to enter a different life we wanted but did not know we wanted. Hudnut's Calvinism is evident in the governing conviction that there is no particle of our life that is not available for God's call. And all of this in a culture increasingly aimed against serious hearing.

The risk of this book is that it will get lost in the shuffle of the current torrent of books on spirituality. But it refuses that genre, because Hudnut understands too well for that. I expect it is a book for new Christians who will here find ways to understand their call. But it is nonetheless a book for old, jaded Christians—people like me—and perhaps especially seminarians who make the call too ecclesial and not enough evangelical. The very reading of the book is from-grace-to-grace. Hudnut writes out of a largeness of faith, and reading the book is an access point for being graced. It is, of course, possible that we may be fated, as Isaiah said, not to hear the call:

> "Keep listening, but do not comprehend;
> keep looking, but do not understand."
> Make the mind of this people dull,
>   and stop their ears,
>   and shut their eyes,
> so that they may not look with their eyes,
>   and listen with their ears,
> and comprehend with their minds,
>   and turn and be healed. (Isaiah 6:9-10)

Robert Hudnut thinks not. And in his presence, neither do we.

Walter Brueggemann
Columbia Theological Seminary
Decatur, Georgia

Part I

———

WHAT IS A CALL?

1

HOW-TOS FOR HEARING GOD SPEAK

Person after person longs to hear from God, to get some word that their lives are on the right track, or if they sense they are not, to get at least some idea of what the right track might be.

It is a great mystery how God speaks. It is an even greater mystery that God speaks at all. But there are those across the centuries who have felt that God has indeed spoken to them. How can that same God speak to us? Through prayer? Meditation? Other people? The voice of conscience? The beauty of nature? Of art? Of science? Surely God speaks through all these. But one way in particular stands out from the rest. God speaks through the Bible, which we call God's Word, and in the Bible through the lives of those who heard God speak to them.

It is astonishing, but God speaks in the Bible to ordinary people in quite ordinary ways: a woman praying, a man questioning, another man on a business trip, another woman arguing, persons who are sick, persons who are forgiven. It is all the stuff of life for all of us.

This "all of us" is intriguing. If God once spoke to ordinary people in ordinary ways, then why can't God also speak to us now? We are nothing if not ordinary. We are just plain folks like the people in the Bible.

It may be objected, of course, that the people in the Bible were anything but "just plain folks," that they were the great heroes and heroines of the faith, saints and martyrs who had a direct, personal relationship with God. Obviously, we couldn't hope to be like them.

But we can, or the Bible would never have made it out of the first century.

"How-to" Handles for Hearing God Speak

This book offers "how-to" handles for hearing God speak. What we will discover is that it is nothing more than the events of our lives that enable us to hear the "still small voice" of God. All we have to do to hear God is do what we are already doing. That may boggle our minds, but there it is. All the Bible people did to hear God speak was do what they were already doing. Then the calls came.

A call occurs when God speaks with particular clarity. It need not come suddenly, contrary to the way we normally view the calls in the Bible. What appears to be sudden is actually gradual, as the still small voice becomes progressively more distinct over time. Then, at the right time, when enough events have accumulated, the person called arrives at a listening point. The listening point appears to be sudden, "out of the blue," but it has been arrived at progressively through the accumulation of events in the person's life.

A listening point is not once and for all. There can be many listening points in a person's life. Paul not only hears God on the Damascus Road, the most famous call in the New Testament, he hears God often throughout his life as a Christian. God tells him which cities to visit, which people to see and what to say. On going to Jerusalem, for instance, he says, "I went up by revelation" (Gal 2:2).

A listening point is personal and unique. "The wind blows where it wills," Jesus says to Nicodemus (Jn 3:8). His call could not have been identical to Paul's. Nor can ours to theirs. The Holy Spirit cannot be contained. The wind cannot be controlled. The Bible describes calls for us rather than prescribing for us our own calls.

But if what the Bible describes worked for putting people within calling distance then, it is quite possible it could work for us now, at least generally if not specifically. As we shall see, if Nicodemus was called through an interruption in his life, it is quite possible we could be too, although it will not, of course, be an identical interruption. If Hannah was called through her longing for a child, it is quite possible we could be called through what we are longing for too.

Each chapter offers a different example of how we may receive a call. At times these ways of hearing God may even be in tension with one another. For example, a call may come at a time of failure or uncertainty or at a time of courage. Yet these are the different moments in which we experience God. In chapter twenty-three we hear God as we maintain the devotional habit of listening for God in our daily life, offering the example of Daniel. Yet in chapter five we see that the prodigal son's call comes in his very failure to listen for God. In each of these experiences God is at work.

One way to merge the Bible's calls and our own calls is to read this book devotionally by choosing one biblical character each day to live with, see in context, and relate to one's own context. Reading the Bible account and the account in this book can give a feel for how God speaks in everyday life.

As God Called People in the Bible, so God Calls You

As you read through the calls in the Bible you begin to discover some interesting things. For instance, you find that many people in the Bible were called during an intensely negative experience. However, what the Bible people discover to their astonishment is that their so-called negative experience often turns out to be stunningly positive.

Another interesting thing you discover in the correspondences is that many of the Bible people were called in an intensely imaginative experience as they looked for something more in their lives. They were experiencing what Pascal and Kant and Locke identified as that vague sense of unease we often experience, the feeling that we have not been all it was in us to be. We know that life has more to offer, that, as God says to Joshua, "There remains yet very much land to be possessed" (Josh 13:1).

The classic instance of such a call is the call of Abraham, who has the feeling, however vaguely, that there is a Promised Land out there to which he has to go. When the call comes, ignoring it is not an option. Abraham has to go. He can't not go and still be Abraham. As Paul cries many centuries later, "Necessity is laid upon me. Woe to me if I do not preach the gospel!" (1 Cor 9:16)

To hear in the Hebrew means to obey. A call heard is a call obeyed. If it is not obeyed it has not been heard and is not a call. A call is obeyed at all costs. You never count the cost if it is a call. If you have to count the cost, then it isn't a call, at least not yet. In the third section of the book we will look at some people in the Bible who did count the cost and so bypassed a potential listening point.

Abundant Life Is Yours As You Arrive at Your Listening Points

One reason a number of people in the Bible bypassed their potential listening points is that they let the things of the moment obscure the things of God. Ironically, the very stuff of ordinary life that brings us to our listening points can also make us miss them: job, home, school, community, country, health, wealth, fame, power, the good life, "the wild joys of living" (as the poet Keats called them)—all these can deafen us to the call of God.

The things of the moment all too easily become idols in the Bible's word. An idol masquerades as ultimate when it is only proximate. Persons worship idols for different reasons: Life for many in the world today is so good they don't need God, while life for many others has become so bad God is no longer possible.

Once the idols are out of the way, or at least have receded from view, we may well discover that, all along, we have been on the way to wholeness, to salvation, to what Jesus called the abundant life (Jn 10:10). Our "inmost self," as Paul called it (Rom 7:22), has been in the process of being joined to the outer: the be-er, so to speak, to the do-er. It is this fusion that we call spiritual, since it is the Holy Spirit in action. Indeed, the evocative process is characterized perhaps by nothing so much as what Paul called the "fruit of the Spirit"—"love, joy, peace, patience, kindness, goodness, faithfulness, gentleness, self-control" (Gal 5:22-23). In the end we will discover new evidence for the validity of Paul's great statement, "At the right time Christ died for the ungodly" (Rom 5:6).

Whenever events have accumulated sufficiently for us, the time will be right and we will be brought to a listening point. Now could be such a time for you. Just reading these words could be the final grain of sand placed on the scales of your life to tip them in favor of God. The events of your life, in all their positive and negative ordinariness, may have brought you to a listening point where, like the people in the Bible, you can hear the still small voice.

A Call Is a Call to Your Soul

How do we evoke the inmost self so that we can become the whole persons we were meant to be? The inner self is distinct from the outer, with the outer's demands of job and home, paying the mortgage, getting the kids off to school, getting to work on time. The inmost self is what the Genesis writer called the image of God (Gen 1:26). It is what is commonly referred to as the soul. Mary speaks of her soul magnifying the Lord (Lk 1:46). On his entry into Jerusalem, Jesus says his soul is troubled (Jn 12:27). Paul and Barnabas strengthen the souls of the disciples (Acts 14:22). The first commandment is to "love the LORD your God with all your heart, and with all your soul, and with all your might" (Deut 6:5). Hannah pours out her soul before the Lord (1 Sam 1:15).

We need a call to evoke our souls. Without a call we run the risk of remaining on the treadmill of life and ultimately dying unfulfilled and unhappy. We have seen this happen to too many friends, and we want, at all costs, to prevent its happening to us. So we find ourselves asking, in an oasis of reflection at home or at work, "How can I be true to myself? How can I be in touch with my soul?"

You can't, of course. If you were in control of your soul, you would have released it long ago. But you haven't released it. Try as you will, with everything from self-help books and psychotherapists to Bible studies and prayer groups, you haven't been able to let your inner self go free. All these have helped, to be sure, but you are still harried and frustrated about your life. You long to be who you could be. You long for release from the prison of the outer self. But nothing has worked.

Whatever breaks through to free your soul is a call, and where it breaks through is a listening point. At such points in life, God is no longer distant, no longer spectral, no longer impossible to reach.

Therefore, the "study of the soul," psychology, is related to the "study of God," theology. This book shows you how to view your psychological symptoms from a theological perspective. The soul's unease is God calling. As St. Augustine pointed out, "Our souls are restless till they rest in thee."

Your Call Is Heard as a Command

All calls are heard as commands. "Go," God says to Abraham (Gen 12:1). "Go back," God says to Moses (Ex 4:19). "Rise," God says to Paul (Acts 9:11).

A command is a step up from a demand. Demands are placed on the outer self; commands are issued to the inner self. The demands on the outer self are not only challenging, they can also be frustrating, like the demands of the dictatorial boss or the imperious child.

If the soul is kept locked up such symptoms as frustration will only continue and eventually worsen. But this heightened frustration may be just what it takes to bring us to a listening point. Every so-called negative emotion is in reality evidence that we are not being true to the inner self. It is a distant early warning that we had better be true, or our mental, emotional, physical and spiritual health is in jeopardy.

Consequently, our frustration may be viewed as God calling, God trying to get our attention, God evoking the inner self by calling it out through the provocation of the symptom. Such symptoms as frustration and feeling harried turn out to be useful to God as a way for God to remind us that we are standing in the way of a theological imperative. (Perhaps the most admired attribute of the saints is their serenity. They are at peace, the opposite of being frustrated and feeling harried. People who hear God's call are able to handle the usual frustrations of life with extraordinary aplomb.)

What theological imperative? We are called to do . . . what? Should I take the new job? Should I marry him? Should I take the initiative with my boss? Should I allow my twenty-five-year-old to live with me? The answers can be revealed at your listening points.

In the following chapters we will see how various people in the Bible arrived at their listening points. Thumb through the chapters and see which headings apply to you. Are you discouraged? Read about Matthew.

Are you sick? Read about Naaman and Mary Magdalene. Are you afraid? So was Moses. Are you brave? So was Thomas. Are you patient? Read about the incredible patience of the first church that brought it to a listening point.

The lives of the Bible people are remarkably like our own. That is why their stories last. All we have to do to come to our listening points is do what they did—simply go about our lives. Then we too will come within calling distance and, from time to time, arrive, as they did, at our listening points.

2

A CALL IS DIVINE

There is an important question to ask when talking about hearing God call: How do you know it is God who is calling? The Bible assumes it is, but you can no longer make that assumption easily. You can't begin with God. You can't proceed deductively, reasoning from a premise to a conclusion. You have to proceed inductively, reasoning from empirical data to a conclusion. And when you proceed inductively, what do you find? What pieces of evidence begin to pile up?

You Find Yourself on Edge

One piece is that gradual realization that your life is vaguely unsettled. You are in a good job, say, but you have this feeling there may be something out there even better, something you have always wanted to do but never quite gotten around to doing. You are not eating and sleeping as well, which is an excellent sign that a call could be in the making. Of course, your call has been waiting all along; you just haven't been in position to hear. Enough things haven't happened to you yet.

Your vague trouble is the same as John Locke's "unease for want of some absent good." It is Plato's *daimōn,* the thing that possesses you and will not let you rest. It is every person's longing for something more, the impulse in all of us that is always striving, seeking, longing to find the one thing that is "really me." If only you could find it, all would be well. Sleep would return. Eating would be normal. You could get along with your spouse and children and no longer be on edge at work.

The calls in the Bible come to people who are uneasy about something. The prodigal son realizes he is throwing his life away. Moses is arrested by the thought that there may be more to life than tending his father-in-law's sheep. Hannah longs for a child. Paul is riven with guilt. Abraham is unsettled about where he is living, far from his original home. He is feeling restless, uprooted, alienated.

It is this sense of alienation from our inner being that is the first evidence that something more is going on in our lives than we thought. We may not call it God yet. Indeed, at this stage we usually don't. It takes a while to recognize the divine nature of what is happening to us. Events have to accumulate enough momentum before we can arrive at a listening point, a place in life where we can hear God call.

You Find Yourself Drawn to Something

Now, of course, your unease could be building up to a call from the Lorelei rather than from God. The Lorelei was a mythic siren of the Rhine River whose singing lured sailors to their destruction. You could set out in perfect confidence, feeling that this was the thing you were called to do, only to fall on your face.

There was no guarantee that Abraham would ever reach the Promised Land. But he went. Indeed, he did fall on his face at first. He left the Promised Land prematurely and passed his wife off as his sister. But his falls from grace did not mean he should not have obeyed the call of grace in the first place.

You could even say that it might well be a call if you find yourself drawn to do something not *knowing* how it will turn out, but drawn to do it anyway. Abraham went out, the Bible says, "not knowing where he was to go" (Heb 11:8). You can't get much vaguer than that—nor much riskier. But the risk did not matter. The risk never matters if it is a call. The risk always matters if it isn't a call. That's how you know it isn't a call—if you can't take the risk. If you are repelled by the risk more than you are drawn by the call, then you will never leave for your Promised Land.

And that is as it should be. You aren't ready yet. You aren't uneasy enough, troubled enough, drawn enough. Fine. Just continue to live out your life. You're sleeping like a baby and you weigh what your doctor says you should.

You can't force a call. It either comes or it doesn't. You have nothing to do with it. It is objective, external. Its divinity is its externality. *This thing has been working on me,* you find yourself saying. The very language we use is externalizing language. *Something's been going on in me lately. I wish I could describe what's been happening to me the last few months.*

I remember a picture in *Grimm's Fairy Tales* in which a demon is crouched on the chest of a sleeping man. The demon is green and hideous, monstrously external. It has come to take possession. It is, however, perfectly possible for the demon instead to be a daimon, an angel. And what this messenger from God does is come upon us at night to trouble our sleep beneficially. Of course, we don't know that our troubled sleep is from God. All we have is the evidence of a growing inability to sleep. But the evidence has become fairly impressive. Throughout the Bible angels come to sleepers. Dreams have long been viewed as a way God speaks, as we will see in the chapter on dreams.

But the question remains: How do you know it is God calling? You don't—not yet. You need to collect more evidence.

You Find Yourself Taking Steps

The evidence mounts as you find yourself taking steps—nothing dramatic, just a few feet at a time. You make a phone call perhaps. You establish contacts. You begin to network. You talk to your spouse and friends. You consult with your pastor. You share your uneasiness with your prayer group. You find yourself praying and reading the Bible more than you had in the past.

You are surprised at yourself. Ordinarily, you wouldn't be doing these things. Indeed, "this is not your own doing," the Bible says, "it is the gift of God—not because of works, lest any[one] should boast" (Eph 2:8-9). Paul scrupulously obeyed the 613 work orders of the Pharisees in order to work his way to God, only to find that his work didn't work. He was as far from a listening point as ever.

Finding yourself taking steps is not your own doing. Why not? Because you wouldn't do it. How do you know? Because you haven't done it! You may have been drawn to do something different with your life, but apparently you were never drawn enough. That is to say, before now enough things hadn't happened to you to move you to take even the first mincing steps.

My Friend Hears a Call

I have a friend who once was uneasy about where he was in life. He had come a long way, was doing well in his job, had a happy home with a wife and children. But it wasn't enough. He wanted something more.

Eventually, his longing for something more bothered him sufficiently that he found himself making some changes. He went to the right sources, made the right moves, got everything lined up, applied for a new job. "I felt if I were to maintain my integrity," he said to me, "I had to apply."

The word *integrity* comes from the root for *whole*. If he were to lead a whole life, he was saying, if he were to be in touch with his inner being as well as his outer, then he had to apply for the job. The call was in the necessity, the "had to." First came the uneasiness; then the drawing; then the necessity, which is how the drawing escalates into action; then the results of the action.

The results in my friend's case were particularly interesting. "The Lord affirmed me where I was," he said. God had apparently emerged during the process in the necessity of doing what he had to do to "maintain his integrity." But then God had continued in the process by affirming him where he was. My friend discovered that an even greater necessity was to stay put. His first call was superseded by a second.

"Bloom where you are planted," the saying goes. But my friend wouldn't have known that if he hadn't taken the necessary steps to leave. It is a great paradox that what you feel is calling you to go may in reality be calling you to stay. But that is how a call works. It works only through unease and necessity. It was more necessary for my friend to stay than to go. His Promised Land was right where he was.

Of course, it helped that my friend was turned down for the job. But when I pointed this out to him he said that he would have refused the job even if it had been offered. He was that sure he should remain where he was. He was called not to go but to stay.

I have never heard my friend so alive. He was upbeat, enthusiastic, almost as if a demon had been lifted from his chest and an angel had arrived in its place. But the angel could arrive with the call to remain where he was only because he had had the courage to respond to what was drawing him, to go with it, to experience the necessity of it.

But *courage* and *refused* are the wrong words. My friend couldn't not apply for the new job and still be himself. A call has nothing to do with courage, everything to do with necessity. It is not a matter of willing yourself to apply. If you can choose to apply, then you aren't being drawn enough. If you can choose to apply, then it isn't yet necessary to apply. The divinity is in the necessity.

If it's a call, you have no choice. You are chosen. "You did not choose me," Jesus said, "but I chose you" (Jn 15:16). "No one can come to me," he said, "unless drawn by the Father who sent me" (Jn 6:44 NRSV). You have to do what you are drawn to do. It is your integrity. It is your destiny. It is your God calling. As an early Christian named Irenaeus was to put it, "The glory of God is a person fully alive." It is only when we find ourselves answering our calls, whether to stay or to go, that we are fully alive. How do you know it is God? One way you know is that you are fully alive.

You Find Yourself Fully Alive

Paul became fully alive at last. No longer an accomplice to murder, he became a "new creation" (2 Cor 5:17). He was specific about what that meant. "The fruit of the Spirit is love, joy, peace, patience, kindness, goodness, faithfulness, gentleness, self-control" (Gal 5:22-23). When you have the Big Nouns in your life, you know it's a call. Of course, you could have each of these attributes and be an atheist. All we are saying is that you *will* have them if you have been called. They are one way you know it's a call and not a pipe dream.

When you find yourself loving more, it is God at work. This is proof that you are at a listening point, because you are loving in a certain way. When you find yourself seeking the best for someone who is seeking your worst, Christian *agape,* you know it is God because you know it couldn't be you. How do you know? Because that's not the way you love.

It is the same with joy. You may have had joy in your life, but you have probably never had it the way the first Christians had it. "Count it all joy," one of them wrote, "when you meet various trials" (Jas 1:2). We "rejoice," Peter said, at a time of fierce persecution, "with unutterable and exalted joy" (1 Pet 1:8). When you can rejoice in the worst as well as the best, it has to be God; it can't be you, because you have never rejoiced that way.

For the first time in a long time you feel at peace, at least for the moment. Things are working out. You are no longer frantic, no longer in a mad dash to be "successful." You are comfortable with yourself. This is the "peace of God, which passes all understanding" (Phil 4:7). Epictetus put it this way: "Do not seek to have everything that happens happen as you wish, but wish for everything to happen as it actually does happen, and your life will be serene."

At last you are patient with yourself and others. You no longer need to snap at family or friends or coworkers. You are surprised at how kind you have become. You don't need to kick the dog any more. Nor do you need to kick anyone orally at work or at home.

The good was Plato's central idea, complemented by the true and the beautiful. A person was good when he or she measured up to a standard of moral excellence. In contrast, Paul found himself measuring up without having to keep the pharisaical laws. We are continually surprised to find ourselves measuring up, from little things like paying parking meters to big things like filing income tax. We find ourselves worthy of the trust God has placed in us. Paul was worthy at last and didn't have to prove himself any more.

You know it's a call when you are a gentleman or a gentlewoman. Aristotle saw gentleness as the golden mean between the extremes of anger and apathy. It was the opposite of hubris, "the worst of sins [for] the Greeks . . . deliberate, arrogant defiance of the gods by overstepping the limits of human being."[1] Mary and Joseph were gentlefolk. Paul became gentle: "When I am weak, then I am strong" (2 Cor 12:10). It was powerful evidence for God.

You also know you are at a listening point when you are in control of your desires. *Self-control* was used of athletes who sought victory (1 Cor 9:25). It was used of politicians who never allowed private interest to affect how they governed.[2] The Stoics possessed self-control to a high degree, but what was their motivation? To show they were in control. For the Christian it was to show that God was in control, since humans *cannot* control themselves. They were then to use their self-control in service to others.

Each of the fruits of the Spirit is present when a listening point is reached and a call is heard. But then, of course, sin reasserts itself, these nine attributes attenuate and may even be lost, and the abundant life Jesus talked about recedes from view. Ironically, however, the more your abundant life recedes and the more on edge you begin to feel, the closer you are being drawn to your next listening point.

Meanwhile, enjoy the fruit of the Spirit while it lasts. It is a clear sign that you have been called.

3

A CALL IS AUDIBLE

We tend to approach the calls in the Bible the wrong way. We view them as miracles and therefore out of reach. But that's our fault, not the Bible's. All the evidence is there for how to hear the still small voice.

The call of Moses is typical. Invariably we begin with the miracle of the burning bush rather than with the events of Moses' life. But what causes Moses to hear? That is the crucial question. He was born well, or at least adopted well. He was brought up in the king's court. He had everything going for him, every advantage.

So have we. Anyone who buys a book like this has every advantage. Compared with most of the world, we live in a king's court. We have everything going for us.

Moses was outraged by injustice. "He went out to his people," the Bible reports, "and looked on their burdens" (Ex 2:11). They were slaves in Egypt. Moses felt at one with them.

Every morning we read the statistics of injustice over coffee and are similarly outraged. Every night we see them on the news. "Love," said the Anglican bishop Gore, "is the capacity to read statistics with compassion." "Lord," prayed literacy expert Frank Laubach, "forgive us for looking at the world with dry eyes."

Moses took action. "He saw an Egyptian beating a Hebrew.... [S]eeing no one he killed the Egyptian and hid him in the sand" (2:11-12).

We don't kill anyone, to be sure, but we do act when it comes to injustice. We join a political party. We contribute to candidates. We write members of Congress. We may even write a letter to the editor.

Moses took the wrong action, commentators have said. It was precipitate and overreactive. It accomplished nothing in the grand scheme of things, although it may have saved the Hebrew, of course, from being beaten to death.

We have all been wrong-headed at one time or another. Like Moses, we have the defects of our virtues. His virtue was leadership, as God knew. His defect was impetuosity. We often rush in to right wrongs too fast. We are quick to take sides in an argument between the children or see only the justice of our side as opposed to our spouse's.

Moses killed a man. His action produced a commensurate reaction. "When Pharaoh heard of it, he sought to kill Moses" (2:15). He had to run for his life.

We have all run from some foolish thing we did, yet this is how God called Moses and how God can call us.

Moses was in the wrong job. He turns up as vice president of the Jethro Livestock Co., and, we infer, it wasn't for him. After all, when you have been raised in the king's court, to be the number two man in a small business in a foreign country is hardly doing what you were cut out to do.

Most of us have ended up in the wrong job at one time or another.

He was on the job when the call came, tending his father-in-law's sheep.

We spend most of our waking hours on our jobs.

He was older now. Things had had a chance to add up. Event had piled on event. He was married. He had a child.

We are older too. Things are adding up for us.

So what do we have? Eight pieces of data from the Bible plus eight from our own lives. It was the simple data from his own life that brought Moses to his listening point. It is the simple data from our own lives that are bringing us to our listening points. Remarkably, Moses' data and our data correspond. Hence we are in position to hear God call, just as Moses was. Simply put, in order to hear the call of God we are just to go about our lives.

A Call Heard Is a Call Obeyed

Once the call is heard, as in the case of Moses, it must be obeyed. We can remonstrate, as he did. But if it's a call, we have no choice. A call is beyond choice. We are chosen. We have only one job now—to obey.

The only problem is that we can't obey, not on our own. It isn't in the human condition to do what we are called to do without divine help. "I can will what is right," Paul says, "but I cannot do it" (Rom 7:18).

The divine call, in other words, comes up against human sin. "In sin did my mother conceive me," the psalmist says (Ps 51:5), referring not to the act of sex but to the condition of humanity. Our sin is the split between the outer and inner self, a split we cannot heal on our own. We have to be healed. Your call comes in what you cannot do on your own. It is the opposite of good old American can-do frontier Manifest Destiny Emersonian self-reliance. You know it's a call if it is impossible to obey without divine help.

Now this is hardly pleasing talk for those of us nourished on what Carlyle called Emerson's "chirpy optimism" and its heirs, "positive thinking," "possibility thinking" and "positive mental attitude," so dear to American hearts. However, we are in grave danger of overstepping our bounds with all our can-do, self-help talk and frontier machismo. These are fine up to a point, but then they can bring us too close to the sun, and, like Icarus, the ensuing meltdown can drop us fast.

God Enables You to Obey Your Call

But original sin is hardly the whole story. The rest is original grace. Remarkably, it is God calling, the still small voice, that powers us over the continental divide in ourselves to make us, at least for the moment, whole, healed, "saved"—all words from the same root. Hence Paul can say that he and his fellow Christians are "dead to sin" because they have been called by God through Christ (Rom 6:11), whose at-one-ment has healed their split and made them "at one."

Our newfound wholeness means that to God alone belongs the credit when we find ourselves obeying a call. We can take no credit ourselves. That is why the bumper stickers of two decades ago loudly proclaiming "I found it!" (meaning faith) were completely misbegotten. The driver hadn't found a thing. He or she had been found by God. "All that we have done," Isaiah says, "you have done for us" (Is 26:12 NRSV).

Faith is a gift, not a choice. You don't will your belief; you are given belief. There isn't a person in the Bible who takes credit for obeying God's call. They give all the credit to God. Even Job, who comes closest to claiming credit for his faith, who was "righteous in his own eyes" (Job 32:1), ends up repenting and saying, "I have uttered what I did not understand, things too wonderful for me, which I did not know" (42:3).

Luther said, "Faith is our response to God's grace," implying that the gift of grace has to be received, which would be a matter of choice. But nothing could be further from the truth. Luther was converted; he didn't convert himself. He was in a thunderstorm and found himself on his knees, scared to death. Later he was to say, "God does not guide me, he pushes me forward, he carries me away, I am not master of myself."

Free will is a myth for those who believe. It clearly isn't a myth in other areas of life, but it is in religion. The trouble is that if we think we choose God rather than are chosen by God, we become self-righteous. Self-righteousness was the Pharisees' problem. Because they scrupulously obeyed the rules of their religion, they erroneously felt they had worked their way to God. It can't be done. God is not an achievement.

Because faith is a gift and not a work, the Pharisees quickly became the objects of Jesus' scorn. They had it all backwards. The very laws themselves, Paul the former Pharisee was to discover, were what made them lose sight of the fact that God had called them to obey the laws and had empowered them to do so. "The LORD has chosen you," the Bible says (Deut 14:2).

Faith is the last refuge of the ego when it is viewed as an achievement and not as a gift. But faith is the last place where we can be like Prometheus, who overstepped his bounds and took on Zeus. Prometheanism was precisely the trouble with Adam and Eve, the builders of the tower of Babel ("Let us make a name for ourselves" [Gen 11:4]), the scoffers at Noah, the executioners at the cross.

God Is Calling Through the Events of Your Life

The person you married dropped into your life. You had nothing to do with how you met. It was all chance, all gift. You happened to find yourselves working at the same place of business. Your intelligence—it was a gift from your parents, simply the fortuitous juxtaposition of chromosomes. And yes, your failures, your depressions, your crises—they can be viewed as gifts because they are humbling you to the point where at last you can receive your faith in God as a gift from God. "What have you that you did not receive?" Paul asks (1 Cor 4:7). "In this single sentence," the scholar William Barclay writes, "Augustine saw the whole doctrine of grace."[1]

Paul never had faith until faith had him, until the events of his life—from being a Pharisee to an accomplice to murder—had brought him to a listening point where at last he could hear his call. "I have appeared to you," Jesus says, "to appoint you to serve and bear witness to the things in which you have seen me and to those in which I will appear to you" (Acts 26:16). At last Paul had heard God's call. Now he would find himself doing the impossible.

What Is a Call?

Q: What is a call?
A: A call is a communication from God.
Q: How is it heard?
A: As a command.
Q: How do I obey?
A: You don't. You find yourself obeying.
Q: What does that mean?
A: It means God gives you the power to obey.
Q: You mean I don't choose to obey?
A: Exactly. A call is beyond choice. That is what makes it a call.
Q: When do I hear a call?
A: When you are ready.
Q: When is that?
A: When you have been readied by the events of your life.
Q: What events?
A: All of them.
Q: What can I do to get ready?
A: Just go about your life.

Q: But doesn't something have to happen for me to hear a call?

A: Yes.

Q: What is that?

A: The next event.

Q: Something special?

A: No. Just the next event. It becomes special as you look back.

Q: How so?

A: You will see it as your listening point.

Q: What is that?

A: The place where you heard God call.

Q: How do I know my call is waiting?

A: Your call is always waiting.

Q: But how do I know that?

A: You won't until you hear your call.

Q: Will that be my only call?

A: No. Just your first.

Q: What happens when I am at a listening point?

A: You find yourself answering call waiting.

Q: What do you mean "find myself answering"? Why not just "I answer"?

A: Because you have been moved to answer by the events of your life and by God's moving through those events. You can take no credit. You can't not answer. You have to answer. It is beyond choice.

Q: Isn't that just semantics?

A: No. You find yourself at an AA meeting. You don't go to an AA meeting. No recovering alcoholic takes credit for recovering. All credit goes to his or her "higher power."

Q: Does this mean that events and God are moving everyone to answer?

A: Yes.

Q: Then why don't they all find themselves answering?

A: Many do. If they don't, it means events have not accumulated sufficiently for them yet.

Q: When will events accumulate sufficiently?

A: No one knows. All we know is that God is drawing the world to answer all the time. "No one can come to me," Jesus said, "unless drawn by the Father who sent me."

Q: What do I hear when I find myself answering?

A: You hear yourself told to do something you never would have done on your own.

Q: What is that?

A: It could be anything.

Q: How will I know what it is?

A: It will be something you can't not do. You will have to do it. It will be necessary.

Q: What if I don't want to do it?

A: That won't matter. What you want or don't want to do is irrelevant.

Q: But how can I do it if I don't want to do it?

A: You will find yourself doing it. Your call is to obey your call.

Q: How will I know if I'm adequate?

A: You will be.

Q: But how do I know I will be?

A: You don't; God does. If you weren't adequate, you wouldn't get the call.

Q: How will I know the results of obeying my call?

A: You won't. Results are in God's hands.

Q: Why should I want to obey if I don't know what's going to happen?

A: You're going the wrong way with these questions. It's not a matter of whether you want to obey. You find yourself obeying. That's how you know it's a call.

Q: How long will my call last?

A: Who knows? Your questions prove that you haven't heard a call. But they also prove that you could be on your way to hearing one. If we keep talking, you could be at a listening point.

Part II

CALLS ARE HEARD IN
TIMES OF STRESS

4

CALLS COME IN
UPROOTING

Abraham

There is no apparent evidence for how the call came to Abraham. All the Bible says is that "the LORD said to Abram, 'Go' "(Gen 12:1). There is nothing to set the scene, nothing you can point to as indicative of a call.

It is the same with us. We say there is no evidence for God's call. But there is always evidence. It is only a question of whether we can see it, or, in the case of God's calling, whether we can hear it.

A man was walking down a crowded street in New York City with an American Indian friend. Suddenly his friend stopped and stood still. "I hear a cricket," he said. "You're crazy," the man retorted. His friend walked over to a flower bed in front of an office building, and there, sure enough, was a cricket.

"You must have amazing hearing," the man exclaimed. "No," said his friend. "It's all a matter of what you're tuned into." With that he dropped a handful of coins on the sidewalk. Everywhere heads turned.

There is always evidence, but we don't always hear the cricket. God is always calling, but we don't always hear the call.

Let's look at the evidence to see how Abraham was able to hear God's call. It could be that the same evidence is already there in our own lives and that we are in just as good a position to hear God call as Abraham was. That may seem incredible, but if it were, if God never spoke except to people in the Bible, then the Bible would be useless.

Your Listening Point May Be Far from Home

How does God call? It's a matter of position. You have to be in the right place. The place precedes the call. You can't hear God call unless you are in position to hear God call. But that is not as difficult as it sounds.

We are constantly being positioned by time and events to hear God call. It is only a matter of hearing the cricket—at the right time, with the right accumulation of events. We are all on the street, but only some of us hear the cricket. We hear it because we have been attuned to hear it. The symphony can play all night, but if you are still in the parking lot you are not going to hear it.

Abraham was away from home. Home was Ur of the Chaldees, near what is now the Persian Gulf in what is now Iraq. He had been born and raised and married there. Then his father had moved north to what is now Turkey and taken his grandson plus Abraham and his wife, Sarah, with him. Abraham's displacement was actually putting him in place to hear God's call.

We have all been away from home. Many Americans are as far from their original homes as Abraham was from his. Does that put us in position to hear God call? Not necessarily, but this is one of the few pieces of evidence we have with regard to Abraham's call, so there is every reason to think it might well be a piece of evidence for our calls as well.

There can be something potentially creative about being uprooted. Paul finds himself in Arabia. Jesus finds himself in the wilderness. Abraham finds himself in the desert of the Negeb.

There is something about leaving the familiar that opens us to the unfamiliar, as to the cricket on the New York street. It is why a child grows so much on going to kindergarten and why a business trip or even a trip to the hospital can open us to creative resources we never knew we had. We are placed in a new place, far from home, where we can hear God as perhaps never before.

Your Listening Point May Be When Your Parents Have Died

Abraham's father dies. His mother has already died. It means that his original family is gone as well as his original home. He has become a displaced person. But it is precisely in his displacement that he is going to be in place to hear God's call. God is calling us at those places in life where we feel most out of place. Not always, to be sure, but often.

It is possible, of course, that you are not feeling displaced at the moment. Consequently, Abraham's call may not be for you. But one of the other calls may be.

Many people are orphans because their parents have long since died. Being an orphan puts you in an entirely different place than having two parents, or even one parent. There is nothing left between you and death. You are next. That thought places you in a different context than when you were young. This is not to say young people cannot be called. Look at Samuel and Jeremiah, both of whom were called as youths.

What about the displacement we may feel from who we really are? Our mentors are gone, perhaps; our heroes have fallen. But what about our heroes within? Perhaps the image of the wise parent within has receded, and we find ourselves caught doing things we know we shouldn't be doing, that aren't the real us. That could be one reason for drug addiction and antisocial behavior as well as for our own antiself behavior as manifested in a low self-image.

When we feel most displaced, the call of Abraham is suggesting, we can be most in place to hear God call. That is why you never want to run from your displacements. You may be far enough out already. All you need to do is listen for the cricket. But we won't listen, of course, until we feel sufficiently out of place.

A friend of mine lost both her parents and, shortly thereafter, her husband. Out of such radical displacement, with no home left she, a strong Christian, created a home. She went, like Abraham, to a totally new place—Brule, Nebraska, just west of Ogallala. She built a home out of the rugged terrain and cleared a yard that takes her half a day to mow. She feeds the birds and the deer and packs a Smith and Wesson revolver as she hikes to the mailbox a half-mile down the road. She lives among the rattlesnakes and mockingbirds. And daily she creates exquisite jewelry out of turquoise and silver.

Your Listening Point May Be When You Are in Your Early Thirties

Abraham was far from home. He was an orphan. By today's measures he was roughly thirty-three years old. (The Bible says he was seventy-five when he answered the call. Since he died at the biblical age of 175, a simple calculation of 75 over 175 yields 43 percent, which, when applied to the average American life span of 76, yields 33.)

A lot is happening at thirty-three years of age. Carl Jung once said that no one ever came to him over the age of thirty-five whose psychological problem was not, in reality, theological—a problem, if you will, of hearing God call.

It is as we grow older that the problem of hearing God call becomes more acute. Earlier, it was something we could put on the shelf, something we didn't have to deal with yet. But by the age of thirty-three the questions begin about what, if anything, is going to outlast us, and, if there is anything, shouldn't we be attached to it, or at the very least do some thinking about it? It is in questions like those, out of the increasingly radical displacements of our advancing years, that the call of God can be heard. Abraham was in a good place at age thirty-three to hear God call.

And what did God say? God told him, "Go . . . to the land that I will show you" (Gen 12:1). It was an order. It was something he had to do. He had no choice. Remember, your call comes in what you have no choice about. If you could choose, it wouldn't be a call. It would be you, choosing. But this is God choosing you.

I once spoke with a woman in an airport an hour before her plane left. She was going to be with her mother, who had just had a stroke. There was no choice in the matter. The call came, and she went. It was as simple as that.

I think of a friend who moved away to take a new job. The call had come with the inevitable offer he couldn't refuse, and he was off. It was something he had to do. There was no choice in the matter. Curiously, he was around thirty-three at the time. Curiously, too, he had no idea how it would turn out. There was no certainty, only necessity.

As it happened, my friend is jubilant about his job. So is his wife about hers. She had none when they moved, no certainty of employment with her former firm once they arrived. She is now a senior vice president of the firm. It is remarkable how things turn out when you find yourself answering a call. They always turn out because when they are necessary you can handle any uncertainty.

The Coast Guard has a motto: "We have to go out; we don't have to come back." That says it all. There is no certainty, only necessity. Abraham couldn't stay in Turkey and still be Abraham. He could stay and run from his displacements and not be Abraham. He could have chosen that. But if it was a call, then he had no choice. Then he was chosen. Then he had to go. There was no certainty, but that didn't matter. All that mattered was the necessity. The necessity would take care of any uncertainty.

Your call comes in whatever vicissitudes of life are uprooting you, turning you into a displaced person, making you homeless. It is at this point, in this location, that you are at last in place to hear God call, telling you what you have to do, what you can't not do and still be you.

5

CALLS COME IN FAILURE

The Prodigal Son

Stories become classics because you can go back to them and they will always be fresh. The parable of the prodigal son (Lk 15:11-32) is a story about how to hear the call of God, and Jesus tells it by describing a young man's failure.

How do you handle failure? More specifically, how do you find God in the inevitable failures of life? How do you hear God speak in circumstances that seem to prevent your hearing God speak? How do you hear God call when the only response seems to be silence?

We can find the answer not only in the particular chain of events for this particular young man, but also in the way each of us can identify with one or more of the links. That is why the story lasts. There is a chain of events in each of our lives that is positioning us to hear God call. It is bringing us to our listening points through failure.

You Sow Your Wild Oats

A first link in the chain is that the young man "squandered his property in loose living" (Lk 15:13). He asked his father for his inheritance, left home, went to a far country and proceeded to throw his money away in what other translations call "wild living" (NIV), "the wildest extravagance" (Phillips), "reckless living" (TEV), and "parties and prostitutes" (LB).

There is hardly anyone who cannot identify with having "sown wild oats" at one time or another. The saying comes from a European grass known as wild oat, which is little more than a weed and is very difficult to eradicate. So if you sow your wild oats you are likely to end up with unpleasant results.

Such was the case with the prodigal son. "When he had spent everything," Jesus says, he was reduced to feeding pigs in a farmer's field (15:14-15).

The events of your life, including your failures, are reducing you to the point where you can at last become available to God. Like the prodigal son, your failure brings you close to the ground, to the humus, where humility lies. It is in your humility that you at last begin to hear God speak. "God . . . gives grace to the humble," the Bible says (Jas 4:6; 1 Pet 5:5).

You Find Yourself in Need

So the prodigal son "began to be in need" (Lk 15:14 NIV). Need is where God begins. If there is no need, there may be no God. We come to God out of our deepest needs. In the prodigal son's case, his need was financial. He had lost all means of support, except, of course, what he got for feeding the swine. "And he would gladly have fed on the pods that the swine ate," Jesus says, "and no one gave him anything" (15:16).

When life is reduced to its essentials, when we are alone and have failed, at the limit of our resources, close to the ground that will one day reclaim us, then God can speak as never before.

Yes, God can also be distant then as never before. We can be too far from God to hear the still small voice. As a man said to me once, regarding a difficult circumstance in his life, "I can't see God in this anywhere."

A lot depends upon how we have read these Bible stories *before* life has been reduced to its essentials. One method I recommend is called "simple reading." Anyone can do it. You sit down with a passage, preferably just a paragraph or two, and note what speaks to you—or what you find yourself resisting. The premise is that God speaks to us in the attraction or repulsion. Then you carry the word, phrase or sentence with you during the day, weaving it into your daily activities at home and work. I have found it particularly helpful to underline what strikes me and often to write it down. I have a friend who writes the word, phrase or sentence into his datebook; it is interesting to see those Bible sentences tucked in around his appointments and "to-do" lists.

Reading the Bible opens you to hearing God's call in whatever happens to you. Then when you find yourself in a difficult situation, as the prodigal son did, the Bible will be there to sustain you, to remind you that God could be calling you in the very situation that threatens to annihilate you.

Take that one sentence, "He began to be in need." If you read the prodigal son story in the morning, you can think during the day what your needs are and go about your activities with the image of the prodigal son in the pigsty feeding the pigs, close to the earth, reduced, ready for God. The image will work on you, preparing you to hear God's call too. Remember, if it didn't have the power to work on you, the Bible would never have lasted.

You Come to Realize What You Have Done

You might want to reflect on this image instead. The prodigal son is there in his pigsty all right, but suddenly everything turns around. I have had this clause underlined in my Bible for years: "When he came to himself" (Lk 15:17). Suddenly the spiral down is arrested and the spiral up begins.

How does it happen? It happens when his failure has worked on him sufficiently to turn him around. And when does that happen? It happens when he finally has enough of feeding the pigs.

Your friends and family may have been telling you about Christ for years, but it never really took until you found the events of your life had brought you to the point where you could hear. It's all a matter of becoming aware. And the only way to become aware is for the events of life, positive and negative, the particular events of each of our particular lives, to accumulate to the point where we can hear what we could not hear before because we had no need to hear it. Then, when the final husk is thrown to the final pig, we are at last at a listening point where we can hear the still small voice.

That is why we say that the events of life are all that matter when it comes to hearing a call. Nothing more needs to be done than to live out your life if you want to hear God call. The events of your life—positive, negative, neutral—are bringing you to your listening point. In the case of the prodigal son, they begin negative but end so positive they are a story for all time.

A grim story was told to me of a man on his deathbed who said to his son, "I am a failure." But even on our deathbeds, we can hear the still small voice. It is conceivable that it may take until then to hear God speak. It may take events that long to accumulate. Unfortunately, they did not accumulate sufficiently for my friend's father, and he died without hearing God. But all was not lost. My friend himself heard God's call through his own failure, read his Bible assiduously, and became a remarkable witness to the power of a call.

You Find Yourself Confessing

Now that he has come to himself, the prodigal son gets image after image of what he is called to do. Just as he had spiraled down in failure, now he spirals up in success. "I will arise and go to my father, and I will say to him, 'Father, I have sinned against heaven and before you; I am no longer worthy to be called your son; treat me as one of your hired servants' " (Lk 5:18-19). *I have sinned.* Confession is the first step in the classic Christian troika of repentance. Many churches begin every Sunday service with confession.

Everyone always wonders about the elder brother in this story and why the fatted calf was killed for the brother who left home and was a failure and not for the elder brother who stayed home and was a success. His very success was his problem. He had nothing to confess. "These many years I have served you," he says to his father. "I never disobeyed your command" (15:29). He had no need and so he had no God.

You Find Yourself Repenting

Then the prodigal son finds himself repenting. You can confess without repenting. The courts are full of it. You can say you did something wrong but not feel sorry for it. But confession without repentance is meaningless.

Repentance in its original meaning, in both Greek and Hebrew, meant "a change of mind." You are different if you repent. You are changed. "I am no longer worthy to be called your son," the young man says (15:19). It was a 180-degree turn. His listening point in the pigsty had become the turning point of his life.

But what about people whose lives are not changed by their failures? Are we to stand helplessly by while they sink further and further? Remarkably, that is just what the father does. He gives the boy the money. He watches him go. There is no communication between them. He just stands by—but not helplessly.

Why does the son want to come home? Why doesn't he move on to another country? Why doesn't he seek his fortune elsewhere? Because the love of his father is calling him back. It is a metaphor for God and the reason Jesus made up the story. God is calling us back. God is calling through the father. The boy is "called" home. He answers his call by returning.

The story of the prodigal son is one of a series of stories of lostness that also includes the parables of the lost sheep and the lost coin. All three are made up by Jesus to announce the prodigal nature of God's love in seeking and saving the lost. All of us failures are being sought and saved by God. The story of the prodigal son is really a story of the prodigal Father whose love was so prodigious it called the son back.

You Find Yourself Atoning

Finally, the prodigal son atones. He finds himself going back to be "at one" again with the one from whom he had split. "And he arose and came to his father" (Lk 15:20). The confession and repentance are worthless without the atonement, without putting ourselves "at one" again with the one whom we have failed.

But *we* don't do the atoning. God enables us to atone. Left to our own devices, we wouldn't atone. But we are not left to our own devices. That is what is so encouraging about the Bible. It reminds us that we are not left alone, that God is calling us through the myriad events of life, even through our failures, as in the prodigal son's case.

It is the father's love that enables the son to atone—unconditional love, the most important theme in the Bible. It is the father who, "while [his son] was yet at a distance, . . . saw him and had compassion, and ran and embraced him and kissed him" (15:20).

He kisses him *before* his son has confessed or repented or atoned. The son could have been coming back to berate his father for giving him his inheritance when he was too young to handle it. He could have been coming back to invite his elder brother to join him in loose living. He could have been coming back to ask his mother for half of her estate too.

6

CALLS COME IN ILLNESS
Naaman & Mary Magdalene

W*hat stressful thoughts are at the forefront of your mind day and night? What is threatening to consume you with its virulence? What is it that you cannot shake?*

You Feel You Are at the End of Your Rope

Naaman was the commanding general of the Syrian army. He was suffering either from leprosy or some other form of scabrous disease. It was consuming him. He could not shake it. Morning, noon and night it consumed his attention. "He was a mighty man of valor," the Bible says, "but he was a leper" (2 Kings 5:1). His leprosy was to bring him to his listening point.

Being a leper meant being doomed. It brought him stress so great that he was no longer able to deal with it. He had exhausted all his resources. He had come to the end of his rope. But the end of his rope, he was to discover, would be the beginning of God.

Help Comes from the Least Likely Source

Enter a little maid. "Now the Syrians on one of their raids had carried off a little maid from the land of Israel, and she waited on Naaman's wife. She said to her mistress, 'Would that my lord were with the prophet who is in Samaria! He would cure him of his leprosy' " (2 Kings 5:2-3).

Often the only way out of our distress is for someone else to come in. Someone has to intervene. Intervention is a method in vogue for treating alcoholism and other substance abuse. The abuser's family "intervenes" to share their feelings about how the addiction is affecting both the abuser and them.

When we say that help has to come from outside ourselves because we have come to the limit of our resources, we are making a potentially theological statement. God can speak to us through someone who appears in the form of the one who comes to us in our distress. Remarkably, he or she may be the least likely representative of God. God calls Naaman through a servant girl who was an enemy, a captive, a slave and a child. You can't get more "least likely" than that. Yet it is she who tells him about Elisha and how he can be healed.

God calls us through the most unlikely interveners. Several years ago I had my car radio on and heard the singer Elton John talking with the interviewer David Frost. John told how he had been living a dissolute life of drug abuse and meaninglessness until Ryan White, the twelve-year-old boy who had AIDS, dropped into his life. Everything changed, John said, because of his times with Ryan and Ryan's family, as he saw their faith and hope and courage. It brought meaning and purpose back to Elton John's life. It saved him.

Who is the least likely person to bring God into your life? I heard the president of a large corporation tell persons at a prayer breakfast how one day as he was going to work he passed a panhandler, only to discover that he wasn't panhandling at the moment but handing out religious tracts. The president found himself taking one from the shaky hand held out to him, and when he read it later in his office he felt the tears coming to his eyes. The tract was about how to give your life to Christ. He told the audience that he knelt down right there and did so.

God Gives Us the Least Likely Thing to Do

God calls to us in our stress, not only through the least likely caller but also through giving us the least likely thing to do. It is bad enough to take advice from a religious leader of another religion and country. But when Naaman arrives, he is told to do something he would never have dreamed of doing to cope with his stress.

He draws up in front of Elisha's house "with his horses and chariots" (2 Kings 5:9). It is a marvelous image—the commanding general with his retinue before the home of the barefoot prophet. Elisha, however, doesn't even come to the door. Instead, he tells Naaman through an intermediary: "Go and wash in the Jordan seven times, and your flesh shall be restored" (5:10).

Naaman cannot believe what he has heard, but that's how it often is with God. We cannot believe what we are hearing. The call coming to you from the least likely place with the least likely thing to do may be the very thing that is bringing you to God. Even Jesus struggles in the garden with what he feels God is calling him to do. Naaman asks, "Are not Abana and Pharpar, the rivers of Damascus, better than all the waters of Israel? Could I not wash in them and be clean?" (5:12)

He has a point. It makes sense. Often we meet the seemingly senseless signals from God with heightened rationality. The Jordan was small, dirty, ugly. The rivers Naaman suggested were large, clean and beautiful, plus they were in Syria, his native country. The Arabs called the Damascus oasis "the garden of the world." It was so beautiful that a story has it that Muhammad, on seeing it, covered his face and vowed he would never enter it, saying people may enter but one Paradise, the one in heaven.

Elisha doesn't even answer Naaman, and Naaman storms away.

God calls us through our points of resistance. Where your resistance is, there your God is—not always, of course, but often, and often enough that we would do well to look at our points of resistance. The reason Naaman resists is that Elisha isn't doing it his way. His resistance is the last vestige of an ego his illness was helping him shed.

This incident is such a dramatic illustration of how God calls us in our distress that Jesus uses it, only to provoke similar outrage (Lk 4:27-28). His reminder that Elisha had healed a non-Jew drove the crowd he was speaking to into such a frenzy that they rushed him to the edge of town to throw him off a cliff.

We are so resistant to what God may be telling us to do through our holy intervener that we stalk off. But that may be precisely the moment when we realize our anger is the Lord God trying to get through to us. We are at a listening point.

God Reaches You Through Another Unlikely Source

Unfortunately, Naaman is so resistant that he needs another intervention. Once again it comes from the least likely source—his servants. "My father," they say, "if the prophet had commanded you to do some great thing, would you not have done it? How much rather, then, when he says to you, 'Wash, and be clean?'" (2 Kings 5:13) They tell him, in other words, that he is being ridiculous. Who is brave enough to tell you that you are being ridiculous? It could be God calling you through that person.

Their intervention works: "So he went down and dipped himself seven times in the Jordan, according to the word of the man of God; and his flesh was restored like the flesh of a little child, and he was clean" (5:14).

He had taken on an appearance similar to that of his first intervener. He was becoming like the one who first brought God into his life, the little maid, the person who loved him enough, or at least loved God enough, to help him in his distress. Why did Jesus use children as the type who would enter the kingdom of God?

So often it happens that the person who brings God into our lives becomes the person we end up emulating in the religious life. A friend of mine told me that when he was in college another student asked him what it was like to be a Christian. My friend told him all he had to do was to watch a certain Christian on the campus. My friend knew it would work because it had already worked for him. He had become like the one he had watched.

Your Call Makes You into a Witness for God

Then, remarkably, Naaman takes on the character of his second interveners, the servants. He becomes the servant of God because he has been healed. "Behold," he says, "I know that there is no God in all the earth but in Israel" (5:15). He is so taken with the new God (who wouldn't be after having been healed?) that he asks Elisha if he can take two mule-loads of earth back to Syria so he can worship Israel's God on Israel's soil. It would make an astounding witness to the Syrians.

You can't keep quiet once God has intervened in your life. Now you become the intervener. You become the least likely source of God for somebody else. You are the one who goes to another in his or her distress. You are the one who starts up the cycle in someone else's life. You are the one bringing others to God, bringing them healing, rescuing them in their distress, bringing them to their listening points where, at last, they too can hear the call of God.

MARY MAGDALENE

We all have our difficulties in life, and at times they can be acute. Your low point, however, can be your listening point, and that makes all the difference.

Mary Magdalene was a woman, the Bible says, "from whom seven demons had gone out" (Lk 8:2). Just as Naaman had a physical illness, so Mary had an emotional, spiritual or mental one (demon possession being associated with mental illness). We will never know exactly what her problem was, although the number seven indicated that it had been serious or was recurrent or both.

One thing we do know is that Mary Magdalene was not what everyone thinks she was, namely, a prostitute. The only reason she was thought to be one was that her community had a bad reputation, and she is introduced in Luke just after the story of the woman who *was* a prostitute. But there is no evidence for Mary's being what the Bible calls a "woman of the city" (Lk 7:37). Indeed, the evidence points to the opposite. She is listed in the Bible with "Joanna, the wife of Chuza, Herod's steward" (8:3). A woman of such exalted social status as Joanna would not be walking around Galilee with a prostitute.

Mary Magdalene was attracted to Jesus at a low point in her life. The Bible suggests that he healed her of some terrible affliction. We are drawn to Christ at our low points as well as our high. A long-time friend had never been a churchgoer, was a nominal Christian at best, and had had a series of jobs that ultimately propelled him to the executive vice-presidency of a major corporation. He came up to me at a gathering and said, "I can't wait to tell you what's happened." For the next few minutes he told me how he had left the corporation to try his hand at his own entrepreneurial venture, how it had not worked out, how he had had to declare bankruptcy and how he was now being hounded by his creditors.

But none of his story seemed to square with the joy in his face. "I've been on my knees," he explained, "beside my bed." And then he told me how, at this lowest point in his life, he found himself going to the little Lutheran church down the street, and how he had become friends with the pastor, and how they have coffee now once a week, and how he makes the pancakes for the Saturday morning pancake breakfasts, and how he doesn't care for the Lutheran liturgy and always finds himself standing when he should be sitting and sitting when he should be standing but how it doesn't make any difference because he is there.

There is a Hollywood ending, just as there was with Mary Magdalene. My friend now has another executive vice-presidency with another major corporation and is gradually paying off his debts and has found a lawyer to keep his creditors at bay.

You Find Yourself Joining a Group

Mary felt called to join the group following Jesus. "The twelve were with him," the Bible says of Jesus, "and also some women who had been healed" (Lk 8:1-2). First on the list was Mary. We tend to forget that. The twelve disciples may have been twelve for a day or an hour, but the group consisted of many more than twelve, women as well as men, and at the end of Jesus' ministry there were one hundred and twenty (Acts 1:15).

Mary joined the group. It wasn't enough for her to come to Jesus out of her need and be healed and then go back to business as usual. She needed to be part of a group of those who had been or were being healed and who would then pass the healing on. It was how she would continue to hear her call.

There is something about joining, about being part of the group, that keeps the healing healing. I belonged to a group of four adults and four teenagers in a church I served. We met every couple of weeks in one of the homes. One night it got a little tough for one of the teens. Her mother had been killed in an auto accident by a drunk driver some months before. She left the group and went into the living room. Then one by one the rest of the group left to be with her. We found her with her back against a piano leg. Everyone reached out to her and held her and we prayed.

You Find Yourself Supporting the Group

Mary felt called to support the group. She gave money to Jesus to help keep the group going. Mary was one of the women, the Bible says, who "provided for them out of their means" (Lk 8:3). We tend to forget that too. It was prominent women of means such as Mary Magdalene and Joanna who provided the money to keep the first church alive.

I think of a teenager who knocked on my office door and handed me a roll of bills. He said they were from his after-school earnings.

"It's a lot of money," I said.

"I know," he said. "It can do a lot of good. I know you'll find a way." After he left, I counted the bills. They came to $100.

Two weeks later there was another knock on my door. It was the same young man. "Here's some more," he said. It was another large wad of bills.

"You're amazing," I said.

"No," he said, "God is."

After he left, I counted the bills. They came to another $100.

We can all come to a group out of need, but it takes the supporters like Mary Magdalene and the young man to keep the group going. Even if we don't agree with everything going on in the group, as she probably didn't and as I know my young friend didn't, our "providing for each other out of our means" sustains the group and keeps it doing what the Lord is calling it to do.

You Find Yourself Staying with the Group

Mary also felt called to stay with the group. She went all the way. Many join, some support, but few remain steadfast to the end. It was Mary who was among the few at the crucifixion (Lk 23:49).

Not everyone had the same staying power. In Matthew, none of the twelve disciples is at the crucifixion at all, only the women disciples, with Mary specifically mentioned (Mt 27:56). The one with the greatest needs is the one with the greatest staying power. In Mark it is the same (Mk 15:40). In Luke and John, again it is the women who are mentioned, plus one of the twelve in John (Jn 19:25-26). And it is Mary, according to John, to whom the risen Christ appears first. She arrives at the tomb alone between 3:00 and 6:00 in the morning, while it is still dark (Jn 20:1). According to the other Gospels, other women are with her, but she is always listed first.

To what can we attribute this astonishing development, that the woman from whom seven demons had been cast out should be the one to whom Jesus appears first in the resurrection? The answer can only be love. She loved him so much that she was the one who was with him at the end, just as she had been at the beginning. And he loved her so much that he appeared first to her.

She doesn't recognize him at first. Maybe it's because of the dim light; maybe it's because of her tears. When she does recognize him, Jesus says gently, "Do not hold me" (Jn 20:17). We cannot, finally, hold the one we love, for he or she will one day die.

Jesus tells her to tell others about him. The way he keeps on living is by our telling. The way he keeps on calling is by our doing the calling for him. Our call is to be there for others in their need, so that their low points can also become listening points. Jesus lives as we love so much that we tell those in need about the One who can meet their need. Then they too may be moved to join the group, to support it and to stay with it.

But would we know that Jesus lives as we love if we had not found ourselves being honest about our needs and joining others in need and supporting them and going all the way with them?

7

CALLS COME IN CRISIS
Gideon

*I*f we assume that God calls us at the listening points of life, the question then becomes, How do we arrive at a listening point? If we say that the events of life have to bring us there, what events are we talking about? Aren't some events more likely to bring us to a listening point than others?

How Are You Feeling Violated?

If we look at the story of Gideon from around 1100 B.C., we find some answers. In the first place, Gideon and the rest of the country were in a crisis. No sooner had the Israelites grown their crops than nomadic tribes from the east, vastly superior in numbers, would settle on the land, eat all they could, and pack off the rest. It had happened repeatedly, year after year, with the nomads coming from as far as two hundred miles by camel.

One place to begin, then, if we want to arrive at a listening point, is to reflect on how we may be feeling besieged, violated, stolen from or otherwise prevented from enjoying the fruits of our labors because of some outside interference.

It is not, however, quite as simple as that. The Bible is at some pains to point out that the Israelites themselves were responsible for their plight. An unknown prophet appears to speak on God's behalf. "I said to you, 'I am the LORD your God; you shall not pay reverence to the gods of the Amorites, in whose land you dwell.' But you have not given heed to my voice" (Judg 6:10).

Here is the all-too-common story of going after other gods, displacing God as the center of our lives, and making family, country, money, job, college, school, girlfriend, boyfriend the most important thing in life. When we do that, forces from the outside begin to get enormous power over us, they precipitate a crisis and, eventually, they can ruin us.

Such was the case with Gideon and his friends. They had been forced to flee into mountains and caves, and we come upon Gideon threshing his wheat in the cramped quarters of a hidden wine press rather than out in the open with oxen, as was the custom.

Who Is Your Angel?

A stranger appears. "Now the angel of the LORD came and sat under the oak at Ophrah . . . as . . . Gideon was beating out wheat in the wine press, to hide it from the Midianites. And the angel of the LORD . . . said to him, 'The LORD is with you, you mighty man of valor' " (Judg 6:11-12).

Who is the stranger who brought you God at the very moment you needed God? He or she is your angel, your messenger from God, reminding you that "the LORD is with you" and has always been with you.

God arrives in Gideon's life through the sudden appearance of a stranger. "Do not neglect to show hospitality to strangers," the Bible says, "for thereby some have entertained angels unawares" (Heb 13:2).

Can You Recognize Your Angel?

Of course, Gideon doesn't see it that way at first. Most of us don't. He argues with the stranger. "Pray, sir, if the LORD is with us, why then has all this befallen us?" (Judg 6:13). It is virtually impossible for us to see God at first in our crises. Indeed, we are likely to blame God for our being in the crisis in the first place. "The LORD has cast us off," Gideon says, "and given us into the hand of Midian" (6:13).

We blame God for a predicament for which we are largely responsible because we have abandoned God. It makes no sense, but we do it all the time. It is such an ingrained part of human nature that it goes back to 1100 B.C. What is the answer to it?

Can You Do What Your Angel Tells You to Do?

The answer to such projections is action. Gideon is spun around so fast it boggles the mind. "Go in this might of yours," the angel says, "and deliver Israel from the hand of Midian" (Judg 6:14). It is a call, a divine imperative.

The answer to argument is action. It is the only answer. You can argue about God forever, but the way to obey a call is to find yourself acting on what you have heard. Some stranger bearing God drops into your life, challenging you to do something so big you can't believe he or she is serious.

Gideon balks, just as Moses did and we do. "Pray, LORD," he says, "how can I deliver Israel? Behold, my clan is the weakest in Manasseh, and I am the least in my family" (6:15). Of course, God knows that. God knew it all along. That makes the call all the more compelling.

By yourself you are inadequate. That is the point. But with God you are more than adequate. The stranger knows that even if Gideon does not. Your stranger who became your loved one knows you are adequate even though you do not. He or she believes in you more than you believe in yourself. He or she knows you can do whatever it is you are feeling called to do in your crisis.

Gideon says he cannot do it because his clan is the least and he is the least of his clan. But the stranger won't let him refuse. "And the LORD said to him, 'But I will be with you' " (6:16). That is all we need to hear. "I will be with you." One thinks of Paul in his illness. "My grace is sufficient for you," he hears God say. "My power is made perfect in weakness" (2 Cor 12:9).

A Sign That You Can Do It

But the knowledge that God would be with him isn't enough for Gideon, and it probably isn't for us. We need something more, a tangible sign that God will be with us. "Show me a sign," Gideon says (Judg 6:17).

It must be our fallen human nature to put God to the test. Jesus specifically avoids doing so in his temptations, but that was Jesus. Elijah criticizes Hezekiah for testing God by asking for a sign, but he ends up giving him one anyway.

Gideon gets some food and brings it out to the stranger, who tells him to set it on a rock. "Then the angel of the LORD reached out the tip of the staff that was in his hand, and touched the meat and the unleavened cakes; and there sprang up fire from the rock and consumed the flesh and the unleavened cakes; and the angel of the LORD vanished from his sight" (6:21).

It would be nice, of course, to get a sign like that at our listening point, but do not despair. There are plenty of signs that God is with us. How about that stranger who happened into your life and showed you more about God than you would ever have seen on your own? How about the birth of your child? How about any number of confirming signs as you go about the big job you feel called to do? Affirmation at work. Feeling good about what you do. Finding yourself loving more. Having a huge amount of energy. "I am large," Walt Whitman wrote, "I contain multitudes." Aren't these all signs?

Finding Yourself Obeying Your Order

Gideon finds himself obeying the angel. It is clearly a call because he wouldn't have volunteered. He feels called to destroy an altar to other gods. Ironically, it is his own father's altar, and it takes ten men plus Gideon, under cover of night, to tear it down. The people of the community are so incensed by what he has done that they want to kill him.

When did you last take a stand against an alternative god? In many communities we worship at the altar of education. This worship often results in our placing so much pressure on our children that they rebel. Sometimes they even commit suicide. We may worship at the altar of success, indenturing ourselves night and day, year after year, to our employers.

In your domestic crisis, you may find yourself slackening the pressure on your children. Or you may find yourself arguing for as much money for poor school districts as your own receives. In your employment crisis you may find yourself slackening your own pace so you can be more of a parent and spouse.

At the height of his crisis, with the pressure on Gideon increasing, the Midianites attack, bringing with them the Amalekites and the "people of the East" (Judg 6:33). It is a critical moment in Israel's history. Remarkably, it is also a listening point. "The Spirit of the LORD took possession of Gideon" (6:34). The Spirit was in a reluctant leader who considered himself unfit to lead but who, nevertheless, would lead because he was being led by God.

At the most difficult time in a crisis, when you feel most inadequate, remembering that you too have gone after other gods, a stranger may arrive with a challenge—and with a sign to convince you that you are at a listening point. It is then that you may find yourself, at no little risk, calling one or more lesser gods into question.

8

CALLS COME IN
UNCERTAINTY

The First Church & Deborah

O ne of the most dramatic listening points in the Bible was in the Upper
Room after Jesus' death. We can imagine the uncertainty of the
little band of followers. Not only were they dealing with their
grief over the execution of their leader, they also must have been acutely
frustrated over not knowing what they should do next.

One hundred and twenty of Jesus' followers were there. In a post-res-
urrection appearance he had said to them: "You shall receive power when
the Holy Spirit has come upon you" (Acts 1:8). The power was such that
by A.D. 313 Constantine declared the Roman Empire as Christian.

How does the Holy Spirit come?

Your Call Will Come As You Find Yourself Waiting
The Holy Spirit came because Jesus' followers waited. Jesus had told the
apostles "to wait for the promise of the Father" (Acts 1:4). That was all
they were to do after his death. But it would be enough. The Holy Spirit
would come.

Waiting is particularly helpful in a crisis. They were in the crisis of what
to do next after Jesus' execution. Perhaps someone close to you has died.

Perhaps you are in a crisis at home or at work, or you may be in some other mental, emotional, physical or spiritual crisis.

> They who wait for the LORD shall renew their strength,
>   they shall mount up with wings like eagles,
> they shall run and not be weary,
>   they shall walk and not faint. (Is 40:31)

Their strength would come from their waiting. It would come from giving the crisis time to sort itself out and so empower them to arrive at a new listening point and hear a call.

Patience is a big word in the New Testament. John Chrysostom, an early Christian, called it "the queen of virtues, the foundation of right actions, peace in war, calm in tempest, security in plots."[1] It describes the ability to endure when something comes upon you against your will—like a crisis. It also describes the ability of a plant to live under harsh circumstances.[2]

The gift of patience can turn a crisis into a call. Perhaps Paul says it best, giving the distinctive Christian twist to crisis and waiting:

> We rejoice in our sufferings, knowing that suffering produces endurance, and endurance produces character, and character produces hope, and hope does not disappoint us, because God's love has been poured into our hearts through the Holy Spirit which has been given to us. (Rom 5:3-5)

But it's unnatural to wait out your crisis. The natural thing is to be active, attend to everything, call the funeral home, call the relatives, prepare the worship service. Such activity is appropriate, make no mistake. But it isn't enough. It crowds out the passivity, the waiting. Then after the funeral you are back to work; it's business as usual, and the waiting is lost.

That is why we say that when you find yourself waiting in a crisis, your ability to wait has to be God; it can't be you because, left to your own devices, you wouldn't wait. It took a week of weeks plus a day—fifty days of waiting—for the Holy Spirit to come at Pentecost after the crisis of Jesus' death.

"For thee I wait all the day long," the psalmist cries (Ps 25:5). "Wait for the LORD," says another, "be strong, and let your heart take courage;

yea, wait for the LORD!" (27:14). After the waiting comes the revealing. After the patience comes the inspiring. And after the endurance comes the eventual joy.

Your Call Will Come As You Find Yourself Waiting with Others

There were 120 of them, and they were all waiting together. There was power in that. They were the first church, 120 out of 4 million in ancient Palestine.[3] That's one Christian for every thirty thousand people. But it was those 120 Christians, because they had arrived at a listening point, who went out and "turned the world upside down" (Acts 17:6). That's how much power was in their waiting out their crisis together.

"Bear one another's burdens," Paul wrote, "and so fulfill the law of Christ" (Gal 6:2). Waiting together is not the only way the Holy Spirit can come, of course, but it's one way, and a proven one, and an excellent argument for being in a church. They didn't wait in isolation. They didn't separate. They stuck together. And it was in their togetherness that they came to one of the most dramatic listening points in the world's history.

In the Old Testament, the Holy Spirit comes primarily to individuals—to Saul (1 Sam 10:10), David (Acts 1:16), Isaiah (Acts 28:25), the Messiah (Is 11:2). But now that the Messiah has come, something new seems to have happened. The Holy Spirit is experienced in groups of the Messiah's followers. There is a collectivity to the Spirit that was sometimes missing before. Even Paul's experience on the road to Damascus was not a solo experience. He needed Ananias to complete it (Acts 9:10-19).

If you are in a crisis and find yourself going to a church, that will be God already. The number of people who join a church during or after a crisis is astonishing. The Pentecost story tells us that "they were all together in one place" (Acts 2:1). The church members are the ones who wait out our crises with us until our calls have been heard.

Your Call Will Come As You Find Yourself Praying

What were the 120 followers of Jesus doing as they waited? They were praying. "All these with one accord devoted themselves to prayer" (Acts 1:14). That's how they were spending their time in the Upper Room as they tried to make sense of the crisis they had just been through.

If you want to find out how God is calling you in your crisis, pray with those with whom you are waiting. To pray is to wait hopefully. Hope is the "anchor of the soul" (Heb 6:19). Your suffering is producing hope, Paul said.

There were any number of other things the people in the Upper Room could have done. They could have dispersed. After all, Jesus had been killed, and it was all over. They could have organized a political party to take on the Romans or, at the very least, the Sanhedrin, which had, in effect, killed their leader. Or they could have sat around discussing what to do next.

But Jesus had told them to "wait for the promise of the Father" (Acts 1:4), namely, the gift of the Holy Spirit, and they found themselves using their waiting time praying. "All these with one accord devoted themselves to prayer" (Acts 1:14). There is something about group prayer, all praying with one accord, that is powerful. Just experience it and see. If you want to hear the call of God in your crisis, find yourself praying with a group of Christians.

I once belonged to a group that would meet every Friday at 5:30 p.m. on the way home from work. Our only agenda was prayer. We had been meeting for months when a new person joined us. He didn't pray aloud as some of the others did. But there were tears in his eyes as we looked up from prayer. His wife had died not long before. Now he had been drawn to wait, with his brothers and sisters in Christ, for the Lord's call to what he should do next with his life.

His call turned out to be witnessing. He was a quiet witness at every worship service and every major church event and every weekly meeting of the men's fellowship group. His witness extended to his business life as well. The impact he made on people was so powerful it lingers to this day.

You Will Find Yourself Witnessing to Your Call

The Upper Room Christians waiting for their call found that their call was to witness. Their ability to witness was convincing proof of the Spirit. They never would have witnessed on their own. They were not strong enough. "You shall receive power when the Holy Spirit has come upon you; and you shall be my witnesses . . . to the end of the earth" (Acts 1:8).

You know it's the Holy Spirit if you find yourself witnessing to the resurrection. That was what an apostle did. When they cast lots to fill the place of Judas, they were looking for someone who would "become with us a witness to [the] resurrection" (Acts 1:22). Your call is to find yourself moving from waiting to witnessing.

I will never forget the man I sat next to on a flight to New York. He had an open Bible and was taking notes. I asked him what he was doing, and he replied that he was preparing his lesson for the next Sunday at his Presbyterian church in Los Angeles. He turned out to be a vice president of a large corporation and on the mission committee of his church. He couldn't stop talking about the church.

I don't know this for a fact because there is only so much time between Chicago and New York, but I'll bet he had had his share of crises, like all of us. And I'll also bet that he found himself waiting for answers in those crises with that community of the faithful who waited with him and prayed with him and, in the process, sent him out to witness to people like me.

DEBORAH

We have heard exhortations since Sunday school urging us to take time every day to listen for God. But we may not get around to it because of the morning paper, getting the kids off to school, catching the bus to work.

You Find Yourself Listening

Deborah found herself taking time every day. That is how she became one of the great judges, or charismatic leaders, of Israel. "She used to sit under the palm of Deborah between Ramah and Bethel in the hill country of Ephraim; and the people of Israel came up to her for judgment" (Judg 4:5). She would tell them what she had heard as she listened for God.

"I was attempting to express what I saw in a flower," the artist Georgia O'Keeffe explained, "which apparently others failed to see." Alfred P. Sloan saw what others failed to see when he saw that decentralization was the key to the future of General Motors.

What Deborah heard that others did not was the harmony behind the cacophony. The times were falling apart. Israel was under attack. People's lives were in turmoil. They were uncertain which way to turn. They would come to Deborah for a word from the Lord.

Why did Deborah hear what others did not? Because she found herself listening. "Be still," the psalmist writes, "and know that I am God" (Ps 46:10). Do you find yourself listening before work? At work? On the bus? In the car? In bed?

"In the deepest part of the night," said a friend who had gone through a difficult time, "God comes to me saying, 'Trust me. Trust me.'" And that keeps my friend going until morning.

You Find Yourself Telling What You Have Heard

Deborah not only found herself hearing the harmony behind the cacophony, she also found herself saying what she heard. She handpicked a man from a neighboring tribe to raise an army to defeat the attacking Canaanites. "She sent and summoned Barak ... and said to him, 'The LORD, the God of Israel, commands you, "Go, gather your men at Mount Tabor"'" (Judg 4:6).

Often we keep what we hear from God to ourselves. We do it because we are not sure we have heard correctly. It simply cannot be that the great God of the universe has spoken to us. On a twenty-four-hour clock, humanity did not appear until five seconds to midnight. The God of the universe is calling me?

Maybe the key to saying what we hear is to find ourselves being as patient as Deborah and the first church. She sat under her tree in the hill country for years before she summoned Barak in response to God's call. Kekulé worked for years on the benzene ring before he saw the solution and was able to say what he saw. And he saw it while he was patiently meditating in front of his fireplace. There it was, with the molecules arranged like snakes, each gripping the tail of the one in front.

A young man went through Sunday school, confirmation, youth club and weekly worship, but it wasn't until a Young Life trip that "everything came together" for him. At a listening point in the Colorado Rockies, after years of patiently waiting, he heard God speak, and he felt called to tell what he had heard by becoming a Young Life leader himself.

Our calling is to say what we have heard whenever we arrive at a listening point. "How do you do what you do every day?" I asked someone who has a particularly difficult job. "It's a calling," she replied.

The calling of America's churches is not only to build community, it is to heal the world. Community is one means among many to bring that healing. So is saying what you have heard.

You Find Yourself Acting on What You Have Heard

Deborah heard what others did not hear because she found herself listening. Then she found herself saying what she heard. Next, she found herself acting on what she had heard. Her listening point had turned into a turning point.

She appears at the forefront of the troops defending Israel. Barak was her general, but either he was not up to the job on his own, or he was smart enough to realize he needed her along to inspire his troops with her moral influence.

It's one thing to hear God, another to say what you have heard, still another to act on what you have heard. We all have great ideas. We may even discuss them with others. But when it comes to following through on them, we often balk.

A YMCA youth worker found himself in Berlin after World War II. A German boy whose father had been killed in the war drifted into the Y. The youth worker played Ping-Pong with him and his friends—day after day, week after week, patiently getting to know them, listening to them. Then, very naturally, organically, he began to read to them from the Bible and take their questions and then play more Ping-Pong. The young German boy is now head of the religion department of a great university and is one of the world's leading authorities on the New Testament.

I was surprised at a dinner party to hear our host ask, "Why don't we share where we've been since we last saw each other?" The sharing that took place, as each of us told what had happened over the last few months, was so deep that I felt we were at a listening point. There was a hush as we listened to each one speak. As if to acknowledge that we had heard God speak through each other, we held hands around the dinner table and each of us offered a prayer.

Then we found ourselves committing, out of our common religious heritage, to do something together in the ensuing weeks to help the cause of racial justice in our community. We would meet with an influential group of black separatists and struggle for common ground. Our listening point had become a turning point, just as it had for Deborah.

9

CALLS COME IN
TEMPTATION

Jesus

One way to test whether your call is a call is to see if you can withstand the temptation to renege on it. Such temptations are so real and universal that they even assailed Jesus. No sooner is his call verified by his baptism and by the voice from heaven saying "This is my beloved Son" than he finds himself in the incomparably stressful situation of being tempted in the wilderness by the devil (Mt 3:17—4:11).

A temptation is whatever lures you from a call. *That wasn't really a listening point,* you find yourself saying to yourself. *I couldn't really be expected to do that, could I?* Martin Luther, after his call to reform the church, was often assailed by such thoughts and would find himself in an agony of second-guessing. At one point he threw an inkwell at the devil, the mark of which can still be seen on the wall of the castle at Wartburg.

The devil may be thought of as the personification of whatever it is that lures you from a call. The temptation could come from a friend, which is why Jesus calls Peter "Satan" when Peter tries to lure him from what he knows he must do—go to Jerusalem and face certain death (Mt 16:21-23). Or the temptation could come from a spouse who says, meaning only your best, "You don't really want to do that, do you, dear?"

You Are Tempted at Your Strengths

Such temptations hit you at your strengths. "If you are the Son of God," the devil says to Jesus, "command these stones to become loaves of bread" (Mt 4:3).

He had been in the wilderness forty days and forty nights, and the Bible says he was hungry. The natural thing would be to succumb to the temptation to eat. But at the moment there was a higher good than eating. He had gone into the wilderness to reflect on his call, and anything that distracted him from his reflection, even eating, was diabolical. You "shall not live by bread alone," he quotes from Deuteronomy, "but by every word that proceeds from the mouth of God" (4:4).

The devil can be seen in whatever makes us satisfied with the good when we could, and should, be moving on to the best. It is whatever throws itself across the path of our becoming who we are, namely, creatures made in the image of God and thus hearers of God's call. The word *devil* comes from the root for "throw across."

> Then the devil took him to the holy city, and set him on the pinnacle of the temple, and said to him, "If you are the Son of God, throw yourself down; for it is written,
> 'He will give his angels charge of you,' and
> 'On their hands they will bear you up.'" (Mt 4:5-6)

On the pinnacle of the temple, for all to see, he was being tempted to do something spectacular to convince people he was the Son of God. Again Jesus would have none of it and beats the temptation back with, "It is written, 'You shall not tempt the Lord your God.'" (Mt 4:7)

> Again, the devil took him to a very high mountain, and showed him all the kingdoms of the world and the glory of them; and he said to him, "All these I will give you, if you will fall down and worship me." (4:8-9)

This time the devil was tempting Jesus with political power, perhaps the greatest temptation of all because the Jews wanted a messiah, and they understood this messiah primarily in terms of politics, as someone who would rescue them from Rome and usher in the new age of peace. Being a political messiah was one of the things he could do best. But was it the best thing he could do?

We are tempted at our strengths to take a path different from the one we felt called by God to take at our listening point. Your calling is not only a matter of what you can do best, but the best thing you can do. When these two unite, you have a call. The temptation is to renege on our call by using the thing we do best for lesser purposes than the best thing we can do.

The good is often the enemy of the best. We are tempted to settle for less than our best in how we perform, and we are tempted to settle for less than the best in what we attach our performance to. By the same token, the best can also be the enemy of the good. We can be tempted to become so invested in doing our best *for* the best that we become compulsive and perfectionistic and unfit to live with. That was the Pharisees' problem, and we have a lot of modern-day pharisees so devoted to doing their best for their jobs and their families and, presumably, God, that they rile everyone around them.

You Are Also Tempted at Your Weaknesses

Our temptations also hit us at our weaknesses. Jesus was hungry and weak. After forty days and nights of fasting, his weakness would be inevitable. It was then that the tempter arrived.

When we are sick, when we are near death, when a loved one is in trouble, when a friend is a victim of an accident or a crime, then, in our weakness, we wonder about God. When we are down, when we are vulnerable, when we have lost our job, when we have given our job all that we have and still cannot seem to make headway, then the temptation to give up on God is real.

When there is evil, when there is war, when the problems of our cities and country seem insurmountable, when we have exhausted ourselves trying to deal with such problems, then the temptation to think that the world is in the devil's hands rather than God's hands is real.

When we are most vulnerable, the devil is most available. Ironically, Jesus' vulnerability comes at the point of his religious observance. He is hungry after forty days and nights of religious fasting.

All the Sunday mornings, all the Bible studies, all the prayer groups and sharing groups, all the time spent alone in prayer and Bible reading, all the time spent with our families in religious observances at home are there to prepare us for the moment of truth when we are tempted to sink to our lowest rather than rise to our highest. And often they don't work as we'd like. We are as vulnerable as the next person.

Indeed, it is right in the midst of religious observances that we may find ourselves vulnerable. The very image of Jesus in the account of his temptation reminds us we are not yet all we can be, and it is the religious ritual of reading the Bible or hearing it in a church service that brings us the image of Jesus.

The Holy Spirit Accesses You Through Your Temptations

"Then Jesus was led up by the Spirit into the wilderness to be tempted" (Mt 4:1). This sentence is often forgotten in the story of Jesus' temptations. His entire experience is in the hands of the Holy Spirit.

Remarkable as it may seem, our temptations are spiritual. This is why you have both spirit and devil doing battle in this story. If we succumb to the temptation, the devil wins. If we find ourselves not succumbing, spirit wins.

The Holy Spirit knows that temptation may be necessary for a call to be obeyed and for the one who hears the call to continue obeying. For the self to be true to itself, it must be tempted to be less than itself. Each temptation is a spiritual experience. The inmost self is accessed only as it finds itself resisting the temptation to live superficially. Our ability to resist is the Holy Spirit. We can take no credit ourselves. The Spirit is what enables us to evoke the image of God and then remain true to the image.

Once we realize the spiritual dimension of our temptations, our whole view of them changes. They are no longer viewed as Promethean struggles but as opportunities for grace. Clearly it was an experience of grace that happened to Jesus. He didn't deny his temptations. He didn't avoid them. He didn't run from them. The reason he was able to withstand them was that he knew the experience was spiritual. He knew his temptations were necessary to his call.

How does the Spirit enable us to remain true to our calls? We find ourselves moved to pick up the Bible. Jesus beats back each temptation with "It is written"; "It is written"; "It is written."

St. Augustine is a classic Christian case in temptations. In spite of his brilliant promise as a professor, he had led a dissolute life well into his thirties. One day in his study he heard children outside his window playing a game. "Take, read; take, read," he heard them chant. He picked up the Bible, and his glance fell on Romans 13:13-14: "Let us conduct ourselves becomingly as in the day, not in reveling and drunkenness, not in debauchery and licentiousness, not in quarreling and jealousy. But put on the Lord Jesus Christ." Suddenly he was at a listening point, and his listening point became a turning point. He felt called to become a servant of Christ.

So what do we learn from this story? That temptation is always there, that it can be a spiritually productive experience, that it should, however paradoxically, be accompanied by religious observance, and that it can hit us at both our weaknesses and our strengths.

And when temptation comes we have Paul's word: "[God] will not let you be tempted beyond your strength, but with the temptation will also provide the way of escape, that you may be able to endure it" (1 Cor 10:13).

Part III

CALLS ARE HEARD IN POSITIVE EMOTIONAL EXPERIENCES

10

CALLS COME IN
EMOTION

Nicodemus

O*ne of the difficulties in reaching a listening point is that we tend to* approach our religion rationally rather than emotionally. This is not to say we should not be rational about our religion, only that the rational tends to crowd out the emotional. How can the Lord God of the universe possibly be calling me? It makes no sense. It is absurd on its face.

That may be, rationally, but, as we have seen, there are other ways of knowing than the rational. One is the emotional. The emotional way of knowing is going on all the time in spite of the constant attempts by reason to discredit it.

A Chance Event Triggers an Emotional Response

It is this kind of emotional knowledge, we infer, that had been working on Nicodemus, a scholar so knowledgeable about his religion that he was called "Israel's teacher" (Jn 3:10 NIV). It had been working on him so long that, by the time Jesus came to town, he was ready to be at a listening point.

Had Nicodemus not been ready, he would not have been emotionally drawn to Jesus. He had too much to lose. That "Israel's teacher" should be seen with an itinerant preacher innocent of credentials was unthinkable. He was supposed to have answers rather than want answers. That is why he came to Jesus under cover of night.

"No one can come to me," Jesus said, "unless drawn by the Father who sent me" (Jn 6:44 NRSV). Nicodemus is drawn by the arrival of Jesus in town. It is the chance event dropped into his life to tip the scales in favor of experiencing God. John Calvin once observed that "the idea of God is naturally engraved on the mind of man." But the experience of God, the call of God, that is another matter. You may have an idea of God, but you may not know God. There is a huge difference. As Jesus says to Nicodemus, "No one can see the kingdom of God without being born from above" (Jn 3:3 NRSV).

How can you be born from above, or, as others translate, be "born again"? How can you change your thinking from thinking about God to experiencing God? In other words, how can you think emotionally as well as rationally?

Nicodemus, the consummate rationalist, could not understand what Jesus was saying. The reason was that he was trying to understand it rationally rather than emotionally, as a teacher rather than as a student.

John Calvin writes that Nicodemus was responding to Jesus with "magisterial haughtiness," which is how rationalists often respond—including John Calvin, who had a man burned at the stake for disagreeing with him. If you do not understand something the way rationalists are saying it, they will often write you off. That is why rationalists have such a hard time seeing the kingdom of God. They can see only one way.

I recently got a pair of bifocals for work at my computer. I needed the distance for the monitor and the closeness for the Bible. Now I can see two ways, and it has made life much happier—that is, once I was able to leap the psychological hurdle of having to wear bifocals. I groused around for a while until it occurred to me that there are more difficult medical problems than having to wear bifocals.

It is the fallacy of rationalism to think that we can only think one way—objectively. We can also think subjectively. "Truth is subjectivity," Søren Kierkegaard said.[1] He made this statement in the context of taking on the supreme rationalist of the day, Georg Friedrich Hegel, who thought you could think your way to God.

For Nicodemus to arrive at a listening point, Jesus knew, he would have to marry his objectivity to his subjectivity, his analytic ability to his synthetic ability. Instead of only tearing things apart, he would also have to put them together. Instead of being only cool, rational and distant, he would also have to be warm, emotional and close. That was going to be how he would experience God. He was half-way there, and now Jesus wanted to get him all the way.

The Pharisee in You Can Prevent Your Knowing Emotionally

However, Nicodemus had another thing going against him. It was not only his cast of mind; it was his mode of behavior. He was a Pharisee. Pharisees were punctilious about the law. They not only knew it, they lived it—to the letter. One law told them not to look at women in the streets. As a consequence, the scholar William Barclay reports, there were a lot of "pharisees" running into walls.

You can spot a pharisee at once if he or she enters your home and informs you that a picture on your wall is askew. The pharisee will then go over to the picture and straighten it. Everything for the pharisee has to be done just right, and if you don't do it just right then you are just wrong. It would be challenging, to say the least, if you had to live with a pharisee.

As a Pharisee, Nicodemus was inured against surprise. People joked about how they could set their clocks by the daily walk of Immanuel Kant, another famous rationalist. Nicodemus not only could think in only one way, he also could act in only one way. If it were not prescribed, then it was not for him. And yet here he was coming to Jesus. It violated every known norm of behavior. It wasn't planned. It wasn't part of his daily routine.

The Ruler in You Can Prevent Your Knowing Emotionally

There was another reason it would be hard for Nicodemus to hear a call. He was "a ruler of the Jews" (Jn 3:1), one of the Sanhedrin, the Jewish Supreme Court, composed of seventy priests, scribes and elders who had legislative and executive powers as well as judicial. They were a tough lot, tougher even than the Pharisees. They killed James, according to the historian Josephus. They killed Stephen, according to the Bible. And they helped kill Jesus.

So Nicodemus had status and power on the line when he visited Jesus in the dead of night. This means he must have known that there was more to life than status and power. He was drawn to Jesus at the deepest level of who he was, his inmost self; he was a Pharisee who could also be humble, a teacher who could also be a student, and a leader who could also be led. All the structures of his life that he had erected to control his experience of God, to know God only on his terms, were being dismantled by the sudden arrival of Jesus in town.

What was going on? He didn't *know* what was going on, at least not rationally. But with his heart as well as his head, he did know. He knew emotionally what he could never have known rationally—that Jesus had the answer to his decades-long search for God. All his defenses against surprise were crumbling.

You erect all your barriers of rationality against Jesus, but then when he comes to town, when he enters your life through some chance event, the walls begin to fall. "Something there is that doesn't love a wall, / That wants it down," Robert Frost wrote. Everything about our lives, every chance event, is moving us beyond rational to emotional knowing. Everything that happens to us is an invitation to experience God in what happens. Everyone who drops into our lives is potentially Jesus calling us.

"How can this be?" Nicodemus asks about being born again. Jesus answers, somewhat testily, "Are you a teacher of Israel, and yet you do not understand this?" (Jn 3:9-10). One meaning of the Greek word translated *understand* is "to experience." It refers to the knowledge acquired in experiences both good and bad. Beyond that it refers to the knowledge of what really is.

So Nicodemus, out of his control and off his schedule, has reached a listening point where he can, at last, hear God's call. And hear he does. The next time we see him he is standing up for Jesus in the Sanhedrin. "Does our law judge a man," he asks, "without first giving him a hearing?" (7:51). This is no stunning act of courage, however, because it is a call. He couldn't *not* stand up for Jesus. Courage has nothing to do with it because it isn't voluntary. Remember, the risk never matters when it is a call. The risk always matters when it isn't a call.

Then Nicodemus is called again, to help Joseph of Arimathea bury the body of Jesus. He brings a hundred pounds of spices and they take the body and bind it in linen cloths with the spices and place it in a new tomb in the garden near where Jesus was crucified (Jn 19:39-41). Had his colleagues seen him, he would have been ostracized.

Nevertheless, Your Heart Can Still Be Strangely Warmed

There was another pharisee years later who did all the right things, judged other people and was highly educated, at Oxford no less. His father was an Anglican priest, and his mother would set aside one hour every week for each of her children to talk about their education and spiritual growth.

Not long after Oxford he found himself on a preaching mission to America, which ended in failure, along with a failed love affair and failing health. But while in Georgia he happened to fall in with some Moravians, people who knew there was emotional as well as rational knowledge, and upon his return to England he found himself visiting their house church on Aldersgate Street.

Someone was reading from Martin Luther's treatise on the letter to the Romans, and it was then, in the emotional closeness of the fellowship and with his keen mind rationally engaged by Luther, that, as he put it, "About a quarter before nine, while [Luther] was describing the change which God works in the heart through faith in Christ, I felt my heart strangely warmed." He was called by God, and the Methodist Church was the result.

Like Nicodemus, life had taught John Wesley that he could know emotionally as well as rationally, and that made all the difference. The events of their lives had brought them both to their listening points.

11

CALLS COME IN LOVE
Ruth & Paul

One of the most familiar listening points in the Bible occurs when Ruth says she will remain with her mother-in-law, Naomi. "Where you go I will go," she says, "and where you lodge I will lodge; your people shall be my people, and your God my God" (Ruth 1:16).

You Can Love Across Cultures

The extraordinary nature of Ruth's call to love is not always fully appreciated. Her husband has just died, which means she is now without economic security. Having no children, she could either return to her parents' home, provided they were still alive, or she could remarry. Naomi suggests both possibilities, whereupon her other daughter-in-law, Orpah, similarly widowed and childless, accepts, returning to the home of her parents and a possible future husband.

Ruth's call to love is all the more remarkable when you realize she was a foreigner. Her country was Moab, where Naomi had come to escape a famine in Israel. If she stayed with Naomi and went back to Israel, she would not only be homeless but landless. Still more, she would be in a land whose inhabitants hated the Moabites. The Jews had passed through

Moab on their way to the Promised Land, wreaking destruction. Then the Moabites fought back, boasting of how they had massacred entire Jewish towns.[1] So even though there was a temporary peace between Israel and Moab, which had allowed Naomi and her family to flee there from the famine in Bethlehem, Ruth would be going into an alien environment if she were to stay with Naomi, one in which she would be viewed with suspicion if not outright hostility.

How then do you explain Ruth's action in contrast to Orpah's? How do you explain her willingness to give up the safety and security of home and homeland for an uncertain home in an uncertain land?

The answer can only be that she found herself doing something she could not possibly have done on her own. She wasn't willing it at all; it was being willed through her. She was obeying a call. How could she do it? She couldn't. The only possible answer is that God was doing it through her. God was moving her to obey.

Her call is all the more remarkable when you remember she wasn't even a Jew. Her husband and Naomi were Jews, but Ruth was a Gentile. So when she says to Naomi, "Your God [will be] my God," she is saying that a foreigner's foreign God has made such an impact on her that it has changed her life. Her listening point is a vivid example of a turning point, a positive crisis, in which her inmost self has been evoked by God and her life has taken a new direction.

The Events of Your Life Accumulate

But why was there no similar call to Orpah, whose circumstances were virtually identical? All you can say is that the events of her life had not accumulated sufficiently to bring her to a listening point. Of course, you could also argue that they had brought her to a listening point and that the call she heard was to return to her parents. But there is no more story to go on there, so following out such an argument would be fruitless.

However, the lack of a call to Orpah raises an important point. Why consider Ruth's decision a call and Orpah's decision not a call? Why is Saul's order to destroy the city of Amalek a call and Hitler's order to destroy a civilization not a call? Why is my plan to run the company my way a call and your plan to run the company your way not a call? Why is my desire to marry you a call and your desire not to marry me not a call?

The answer can only be in the criteria for hearing the still small voice. Does your decision, order, plan, desire evoke your inmost being, your soul? Has it come to you in the normal run of your everyday life? Is it something impossible for you to do on your own? Is it something you have to do? Does it bring you love, joy and peace; make you more patient, kind and good; help you be more faithful, gentle and self-controlled? If so, it is a call.

Your Love Brings Unexpected Rewards

Not only is Ruth's arrival at her listening point remarkable enough in itself, the results of Ruth's call are equally remarkable. She goes into the fields at the time of the harvest to glean, which involved picking up what was left after the grain had been cut and put up in sheaves. A law stated that the poor, the alien, the widow and the fatherless could pick up the leavings. Ruth qualified on all counts. She was gleaning not only for herself but for Naomi as well, and she was doing so at great risk to herself, being a hated alien and a woman alone in the fields with the harvesters.

"She happened to come to the part of the field belonging to Boaz, who was of the family of Elimelech," her late husband's father (Ruth 2:3). There was another law that made it a duty for a male family member to marry another family member's widow. Boaz could marry her if there were no closer relative who wanted to, thus providing her with a new home.

"She happened to come ..." It is the things that happen to us that can be incomparably graceful, full of grace. "Life must be lived forward," Søren Kierkegaard wrote, "but it can only be understood backward." As we look backward, we can see the hand of God in what just happened to us: the chance encounter, the unexpected phone call, the letter.

Boaz happens to notice Ruth. "Whose maiden is this?" he asks (2:5). He tells her how to be safe in the fields and how he has heard all about what she has done for Naomi. He invites her to share the noon meal. He instructs his men to leave her more gleanings. Soon she is sleeping at his feet, and he is asking the next of kin, who is legally entitled to marry Ruth, if he wants to marry her. When the next of kin says that he doesn't, the way is clear for Boaz as the so-called kinsman-redeemer, the next in line after the refusal of the closer relative.

Who is your redeemer? Who, when you were homeless, brought you home? Who, when you were feeling alienated, helped you feel accepted? Who loved you as Boaz loved Ruth?

I have a friend who has no kinsman-redeemer. I tried to be but failed. All his life he has been looking for home, but he has never found one. He was not loved in his first family, and he has never had another family. So he has taken out his loss of love on society.

When I visited him in the state prison, he told me he had been to the prison chapel but didn't go back. "Why not?" I asked.

"Because I didn't find what I was looking for."

"What was that?"

"Love."

What about your ultimate redeemer and your eternal home? It just so happens that Ruth is the ancestor of Jesus (Mt 1:5). When you leave your home for your eternal home, he will be there. "In my Father's house are many rooms. . . . When I go and prepare a place for you, I will come again and will take you to myself, that where I am you may be also" (Jn 14:2-3).

You Can Love Unconditionally

How do we obey the call to love as Ruth and Boaz did? We don't, of course. Even when approximations occur, they have to be God; they can't be us because we don't love all that easily, particularly if we have to leave home and homeland for enemy territory. God is the force that empowers us to do this kind of loving. "God is love," the Bible says (1 Jn 4:16). Mostly we love conditionally. I love you—if you clean your room. I love you—if you see it my way. I love you—if you marry me.

God has been showing us unconditional love all along, and our recognition of such love at the listening points of life should inspire us to show the same love. The things that happen to us are graceful, full of grace, of God. "What have you that you did not receive?" Paul asks (1 Cor 4:7).

If you are married, God brought you your spouse. You happened on each other the way Boaz and Ruth happened on each other. God brought you your parents. They just happened to meet, and as the result of their meeting, unlike my homeless friend, you happened to grow up being loved and even loved unconditionally.

If you have children, God brought them to you. There was no assurance you would have them, and now you find yourself loving them the way Ruth loved Naomi and Boaz loved Ruth. It is hoped that you find yourself giving all the credit to God when you find yourself loving this way. Your love may even produce the first theological statement of your life: "God is someone I thank for someone I love."

Why not read the story of Ruth at home? Stories connect as nothing else. A conference was held in 1990 of the courageous rescuers of Jews during the Holocaust. It was revealed that only one person out of every four hundred who could have rescued did. That means that, out of fifty thousand people in a given city, only 125 would dare to do anything for the Jews. That is how rarely we are able to love unconditionally. Tell the stories of the rescuers, the conference concluded. That is how you will educate your children morally.

It is also how you will educate them theologically. God becomes real in the stories of the calls and in the other Bible stories. The God of Ruth is a God of deeds, of drama, of story. As the great Jewish theologian Abraham Joshua Heschel put it: "We have no nouns by which to describe God's essence; we only have adverbs by which to indicate the ways in which God acts toward us."[2] One of those ways, the supreme way, is to love us unconditionally. Another is to call us continually.

PAUL

There are only two bottom-line emotions, the negative one of fear and the positive one of love. Which predominates in your life?

All Too Often, Fear Beats Love

We let our fears get the better of us all too often. We are afraid of advancing age, afraid of retirement, afraid of bad health, afraid of failure, afraid of other people, afraid of financial ruin, afraid of bad grades at school. Our lives are often governed by our fears.

It certainly seemed so for Paul. Pharisees were so afraid of being on the wrong side of God that they separated themselves from everyone else.

In fact, their name means the "separated ones". They thought their 613 rules for living could beat their fears. They were wrong, as Paul would be the first to attest.

We erect all sorts of defenses against our fears, from displacing onto others what we are afraid of to becoming judgmental, critical, hard to live with. You can always identify people whose bottom line is fear rather than love because you feel worse after being with them.

A classic defense against fear is to keep busy. That way our fears can't reach us. We become human doings instead of human beings. As such, we feel we can control our fear. If we can just pack 613 things into our week, there will be no time for fear to take over. We can keep it at bay. When we are in bed, of course, it's another matter, and we often sleep fitfully or with nightmares.

Or we defend against fear by sticking with our own. We separate into tight little islands of sameness called suburbs. We become tribal and separate from other tribes, the disastrous effects of which can be seen not only in the neglect of our inner cities but in the war zones of Kosovo, Rwanda and elsewhere. If I can associate with "my own," I will be safe. I will have nothing to fear.

When I was in seminary in New York, I did my fieldwork in Harlem. It was the first time I had been separated from my tribe. As the parish visitor for one of the churches in the East Harlem Protestant Parish, my job was to call on the families in the "projects," the public housing units near the church. I discovered that East Harlem was so tribal that members of the tribe would have to walk me, a member of the Upper West Side tribe, to a cab at night so I would not be attacked.

Church is another way we defend against fear. We squeeze the tribe down to one room. Everyone inside the room is safe; everyone outside the room is unsafe, "damned," "going to hell," or is otherwise pharisaically separated out as "impure," not "one of us."

What we should be doing, of course, is trying to find the common ground underlying all religions so we can all be forbearing toward one another and even appreciate one another. Finding such common ground is the only hope for world peace, since so many of the current or recent wars involve religion: Catholic versus Orthodox in Croatia and Serbia,

Orthodox versus Muslim in Bosnia and Herzegovina, Protestant versus Catholic in Northern Ireland, Muslim versus Christian in Sudan. Crusades are going on all over the world in the name of my tribe versus your tribe.

With the Call of Christ, Your Love Can Beat Your Fear

Fortunately, there is a lot more going on in us than fear, namely, love. *Love Is Letting Go of Fear* is the title of a remarkable little paperback written by Gerald Jampolsky, a psychiatrist who makes his living with dying children. It is also the basic message of the Bible. "There is no fear in love," the Bible says, "but perfect love casts out fear" (1 Jn 4:18).

The bottom-line positive emotion is love, a deeper emotion than fear, and until that emotion was released Paul never really got going in his life. Indeed, he was going backwards because of his persecution of those who disagreed with his way of handling his fears. Even as a Christian he could write, "I do not do the good I want, but the evil I do not want is what I do. ... Wretched man that I am! Who will deliver me from this body of death? Thanks be to God through Jesus Christ our Lord!" (Rom 7:19, 24-25).

The only way he could move from being a killer to a lover was for the call of Jesus Christ to interdict the downward spiral of his life. The only way he could handle his fears was to find them being handled by Jesus. And the only way he could find the God for whom he was searching was to be found by that God on the road to Damascus in an experience of the risen Christ.

Paul was so defended against God by trying to handle his fears on his own that God had to break through his defenses. "Batter my heart, three-personed God," John Donne wrote. A similar battering may have to happen to us if we are very critical, very scheduled, and very tribal. "God is love" (1 Jn 4:16), as we have seen in the calls of Ruth and Mary Magdalene. But we cannot know this if we are defended against it by living out of fear.

God has to break through to us. We need some sort of experience like Paul's if we are to live our lives out of love and not out of fear. The fascinating thing about Paul's experience was that he had nothing to do with it. He was simply going about business as usual, on his way to Damascus to round up Christians for jail and execution. Then came the bold interdiction.

There is something immensely hopeful about Paul's experience. It suggests that we don't have to do anything to have it. There is no 614th law for scheduling an experience of Jesus and thus finding our love beating our fear. The Bible's suggestion is that whenever we find ourselves loving, that is of God. When Jesus said, "I am the way, and the truth, and the life" (Jn 14:6), he was saying, among other things, that the way of love is the way of God, and he himself was incarnating it.

The way of love includes the way of truth, but the way of truth does not necessarily include the way of love. When it is simply the way of truth, then it is my truth versus your truth, and if you don't accept my truth, then I can shut you out of my room. I can even go into your room and throw you out. But if my truth is love, then I open the doors of my room to you. I invite you in by loving you, by incarnating "God is love." The Bible does not say "God is truth," but "God is love." Love is the truth. The truth about God is love.

Love is the only fundamental. The trouble with the Pharisees was that they put truth above love. But the trouble with truth's being the only fundamental is that it has an alarming tendency to eliminate love. If you don't salute my truth, then I can eliminate you, as happened all too easily in the Crusades, the Inquisition, Nazi Germany, the McCarthy hearings, and is happening in war after war today. Such pharisaism is arrogant, whether it be religious, political, familial, cultural, national, or philosophical.

Jesus loved everyone. We would do well to stop playing God and start playing Jesus.

When the Serbian center for the Los Angeles Lakers, coming from an Eastern Orthodox culture, met the Croatian guard for the New Jersey Nets, coming from a Catholic culture, at the Forum in Inglewood, California, he publicly snubbed his former teammate on the Yugoslav National Team. That is pharisaism, and when it takes the form of nationalism or racism or narcissism or dogmatism of any form, it is invariably hostile to love.

You Find Yourself Loving the Very People You Feared

All of a sudden the Pharisee Paul finds himself loving the people he has been killing. It is one of the most dramatic reversals in history. His experience of the call of Jesus throws him over into the rest of who he is—a human being as well as a human doing, someone with an inner as well as an outer self. His call enables him to tap into that deeper reservoir of who he is, where love is deeper than fear.

Jesus, the incarnation of love, gains the access to love for us. That is why Christianity is such a powerful religion and why the cross, the symbol of the ultimate in love, is such a powerful symbol.

"Repent," Jesus said in his first sermon (Mk 1:15). Repent of your schedule that schedules you in and God out. Repent of your tribalism that keeps you and others like you in, and everyone else out. Repent of your projections and persecutions and dogmatisms and all the other defenses you throw up against the release of the lover in you.

But we don't repent. We won't repent. We can't repent. It was one of Jesus' impossible commands. He knew we couldn't repent, just as God knew Paul couldn't. He knew it would have to be God moving us to repent. When you find yourself repenting, that is God in your life. When you find yourself loving, that is God. God *is* love. God does what we cannot do, by definition.

Before he died, Lee Atwater, the former Republican Party chairman, who had made a habit of savaging those he felt were his enemies, wrote an apologetic letter to each. Senator James Eastland, the archconservative segregationist from the South, did the same before he died. Charles Colson, who said he would walk over his own grandmother for President Nixon, repented of his involvement in Watergate and now has a prison ministry throughout the country. In each case, it was their encounter with Christ, like Paul's, that led them to repent of a life of fear and to embark on a life of love.

12

CALLS COME IN RELATIONSHIPS

Andrew & Philemon

Nobody remembers *Andrew, but without Andrew we might never have* had Peter, because it was Andrew who introduced Peter to Jesus. According to the Gospel of John, Andrew "brought him to Jesus" (Jn 1:42). Andrew had responded to the call of John the Baptist, but when John met Jesus and said, "Behold, the Lamb of God!" (1:36), Andrew found himself leaving John for Jesus, asking Jesus where he was staying, and then remaining with him from late afternoon through the rest of the day.

Afterwards, the first thing Andrew did was run with the excitement of his discovery to his brother. "He first found his brother Simon, and said to him, 'We have found the Messiah'. . . [and he] brought him to Jesus" (1:41-42).

It's all a matter of who brings us to Jesus, and then, of course, it's a matter of whom we will bring.

Who Brings You to Jesus?

In my case, and of necessity we have to be autobiographical in such matters, the first people who brought me to Jesus were my parents. I was one of those fortunate people who had parents who were already Christians and who took the faith seriously enough to make it a regular part of family life.

Every night my mother would read to us from a big blue Bible storybook, which had a large picture filling the right-hand page. To this day, all six of her children can describe in detail virtually every picture in the book, and there are a hundred of them for a hundred of the most important stories in the Bible.

My father also brought us to Jesus every morning. He would read a story at breakfast, from either the Bible or a book of children's sermons, and he would read with great sensitivity, sometimes even through tears. Then he would offer a prayer before we ate.

Whichever parent put us to bed would always pray with us, and their praying continued until we reached junior high school.

In addition, when I was thirteen, my father gave me a treasure, a pocket New Testament, which he had inscribed with a quotation from 2 Timothy: "Keep the great securities of your faith intact" (2 Tim 1:14 Moffatt). I would read from my new Bible every night, keeping it on the bedside table beside a cross my parents had given me, which glowed in the dark as I went to sleep.

As a teenager I had asthma, so I was sent to the clear air provided by a boarding school high in the Smoky Mountains outside of Asheville, North Carolina. There I met the chaplain, the third person to bring me to Jesus, my third Andrew. A man of rocklike integrity, he was massively impressive to all the students, universally liked as well as respected. When he spoke in chapel on Sunday morning or during the week, he had not just a captive audience but a captivated one.

At college, I had a pivotal experience in the first few weeks of my freshman year. Two students from a nearby seminary began to visit the campus and gradually came to know several freshmen, one of whom was my roommate. They began small group meetings once a week. These meetings meant so much to my roommate that he did for me what Andrew did for Peter. "Come and see," he said, and I went to one of the meetings.

There was a brief reading from the Bible, but mostly we shared experiences and prayed. It was my first experience of a koinonia group and proved to be so dynamic that my roommate and I both went into the ordained ministry, while a third roommate went on to become a lay leader in his church.

I recall another significant memory from college. During my sopho- more year, I had a roommate who would kneel beside his bed every night before going to sleep. I was most impressed. He would also go to church every Sunday without fail.

When senior year rolled around, I had to figure out what I was going to do with my life. It just so happened, as such things do, that the assistant chaplain at the college told me about a fellowship that would take me to any seminary in the country for one year to think about whether the ordained ministry might be for me. I remember going up to the New York Life Insurance Company in New York City for my interview and having the people sitting around the big table in the boardroom fire questions at me.

Then a curious thing happened. Long before seminary opened in the fall, I received a letter from one of the Old Testament professors welcom- ing me to the seminary. My brother was already there, and he must have mentioned that I had been accepted. But this was no ordinary letter. It touched me in my inmost self. I was to become one of this professor's most ardent admirers and later even dedicated one of my books to him.

Midway through that trial year at seminary I was accepted as a Ph.D. candidate at Harvard, and I had to make the toughest decision of my life—whether to stay in the seminary or leave for the university. I talked it over with four professors, including my Old Testament friend, and with the help of these four Andrews I decided to stay at the seminary and so remain close to Christ through my profession as well through other aspects of my life. Life in Christ is a series of Andrews who happen into our lives and bring us to Jesus.

Whom Do You Bring to Christ?

After answering Jesus' call, "Come and see" (Jn 1:39), Andrew finds himself issuing the call on Jesus' behalf, telling his brother, "We have found the Messiah" (1:41). But he doesn't leave it at that. He takes the next step: "He brought him to Jesus" (1:42).

Statistics on church membership are revealing: 3 percent join a church because of its program, 5 percent because of the church school, 6 percent because of the pastor, 7 percent for other reasons, and a whopping 79 percent because a relative or friend brought them, as Andrew brought Peter.

Many denominations are experiencing serious membership losses, and have been for years. One reason can only be that their members are not as excited about their calls as Andrew was about his. When he runs home and tells his brother, "We have found the Messiah," he is saying that he has found the one who brings love, joy, peace, meaning and purpose into his life. Then he brings his brother to Jesus. He was that excited about what he had found, or, more accurately, about what had found him.

That next step, of actually bringing someone to church or to a small group or to a fellowship of Christians, is the crucial one in determining whether we have heard the call of Christ.

PHILEMON

Paul issues a call to his friend Philemon to take back his runaway slave, Onesimus, without the usual punishment—branding on the forehead with the letter "F" (from the Latin for "flee") or crucifixion. Theirs is a close friendship. "I have derived much joy and comfort from your love," Paul writes (Philem 7). "Prepare a guest room for me," he adds at the letter's end (v. 22). Your call may be coming to you through someone close enough to you to be your houseguest.

Furthermore, they are both Christians. Paul calls Philemon his "beloved fellow worker" (v. 1). He is a particularly effective worker. For one thing, the church meets in his home. Paul sends greeting to "the church in your house" (v. 2).

For another thing, Philemon shares his faith with others. "I pray that the sharing of your faith," Paul writes, "may promote the knowledge of all the good that is ours in Christ" (v. 6). "The hearts of the saints have been refreshed through you" (v. 7). This is no nominal Christian. Philemon is a mature disciple.

You Have Been Seriously Wronged

Accordingly, to use Paul's word (Philem 8), you are in an excellent position to be called by God through an even more mature Christian who is one of your closest friends. He or she will be suggesting you do something you know you should do to someone who has wronged you.

Onesimus, the runaway slave, had seriously wronged Philemon. Slaves were property. He had stolen Philemon's property. On top of that, he had stolen money from Philemon to finance his getaway, a sum that Paul offers to pay back (vv. 18-19).

Christian love, or *agape*, the word Paul uses here (v. 5), seeks the best for someone who is seeking your worst. To do so is a tall order, and Paul is asking Philemon to fill it. "I appeal to you for my child, Onesimus" (v. 10). Because Philemon is such a good Christian, he, of all people, is in position to hear such a call—if, of course, time and events have brought him to the point where he can.

The experts are careful to point out that we should not view Paul's letter anachronistically. The culture was not ready for Paul to ask Philemon to free Onesimus, only to welcome him back. The time had not yet come to do anything about the institution of slavery. Indeed, working to free slaves, at this point in time, would have worked against eventual release by their owners and against this particular owner's receiving Onesimus back mercifully rather than punitively.

The society was built on slavery. Aristotle had described it as being "in the nature of things,"[1] just as segregation in our own society used to be in the nature of things—and smoking, and women working only in the home, and noninclusive language, and lack of concern for the environment.

Perhaps someone had recognized Onesimus as a runaway slave, so something had to be done.[2] Just such chance occurrences in life are crucial to our development as hearers of the call. If time and events enable the chance event to register on the inmost self, then we are at a listening point. If they don't, then we aren't.

Paul is hopeful that the chance event of his letter and the return of Onesimus, the bearer of the letter, will register as a call to Philemon. He tries to make sure that they will by couching his call as an "appeal" (v. 8) rather than a "command" (v. 9), hoping that Philemon will thus be moved to hear it as a call and hence something he must obey.

Your call, in other words, will come when a close and mature Christian friend appeals to you on behalf of someone who has wronged you.

The One Who Has Wronged You Is Also a Christian

A new factor comes into play. Onesimus is a Christian. "I appeal to you," Paul writes, "for my child, Onesimus, whose father I have become in my imprisonment" (Philem 10).

After fleeing Philemon, Onesimus has become a Christian under Paul's tutelage, and it has changed his life. The word *onesimus* means "useful" in Greek, and Paul puns on the word by writing "Formerly he was useless to you, but now he is indeed useful to you and to me" (v. 11). As a Christian and a slave, Onesimus can be a powerful witness for Christ.

What Paul is doing, then, is asking Philemon to receive Onesimus as a fellow Christian. "Receive him as you would receive me," he writes (v. 17). They would no longer be slave and master but fellow slaves of Christ. Early Christians used the word *slave* to describe themselves (Rom 1:1, Jude 1:1). Slaves had no will of their own. As Paul put it, "to me to live is Christ" (Phil 1:21). "My conscience is captive to the will of God," Luther said.

Philemon and Onesimus were slaves of the same master, and that made all the difference. "My very heart," Paul calls Onesimus (Philem 12). Then he adds, "Perhaps this is why he was parted from you for a while, that you might have him back for ever, no longer as a slave but more than a slave, as a beloved brother" (vv. 15-16).

Let's say the person who wronged you is a Christian. As servants of the same master you have more that unites than divides you. All that is necessary is for you to respond to the call of a close Christian friend to seek the other's best even though he or she was seeking your worst.

Perhaps it is someone in your own family who has wronged you, or someone at work or a friend. Perhaps the two of you are no longer talking. Maybe it is years since you have been in touch. But maybe this is why you were parted from each other, that you might have each other back forever, as Christians, because you were willing to forgive. Doesn't it put your relationship on an entirely new plane, that you are both Christians, no longer just a brother or sister or parent or child or friend or boss or employee, but a beloved brother or sister in Christ?

The One Who Wronged You Can Be Transformed

It is fifty years later. One of the early Christian leaders, Ignatius, is being led through Asia Minor on his way to martyrdom in Rome. He writes letters the churches on his way. Ogne is to the church in Ephesus. He speaks highly of the bishop of Ephesus. He calls him "a man of inexpressible love." "I pray . . . that you would all be like him," he writes. Then he adds, "Blessed be He who has granted unto you . . . to obtain such an excellent bishop."[3]

The bishop's name? Onesimus. We will never know for sure, but the bishop could well have been Paul's "very heart."

The useless one had become useful indeed, and all because Philemon had found himself at a listening point, responding to the call of God to seek the best for someone who had sought his worst, as that call came to him through a beloved Christian friend.

13

CALLS COME IN COURAGE

Thomas

Most of us at one time or another are assailed by doubts about God, Jesus, hearing a call and many other aspects of the spiritual life. We have a lot more going for us in our doubts than we may think.

An article appeared in the magazine *Science* in which the noted astrophysicist Paul Davies staged an argument between a hypothetical man of science and a hypothetical man of faith—the two sides of himself, no doubt. The results, however, were not encouraging. The two simply agreed to disagree.

We see the same two sides in Thomas, although most of us remember only one, the so-called "Doubting Thomas" side. Of all the disciples, he needed the evidence, the empirical data, for the spiritual life. What we forget is that the data were accumulating for Thomas all along. He was being prepared by life for his great pronouncement about Jesus, "My Lord and my God!" (Jn 20:28) We are being prepared in the same way.

Your Courage Can Lessen Your Doubt
The first thing we forget is that Thomas was brave. John would not have put Thomas's bravery in his Gospel if it were not important, indeed

crucial, to Thomas's eventual hearing the call of the risen Christ. Indeed, in his bravery were the seeds of his pronouncement.

Jesus hears that his good friend Lazarus is sick, and he wants to go to him. The only trouble is that Lazarus lives in enemy territory, and the disciples remonstrate with Jesus not to go. "Rabbi," they say, "the Jews were but now seeking to stone you, and are you going there again?" (Jn 11:8) Only one disciple stands up for Jesus. But he is so effective that he turns the whole group around. "Let us also go," Thomas says, "that we may die with him" (11:16).

We all have such moments of bravery; they prepare us to handle our doubts when they come and so to hear our calls. As a friend of mine said while contemplating a major change in his life, "You pray to God, and then—you throw yourself out there."

Another friend was about to have a serious operation. She had a living will and did not want the surgeon to take extraordinary measures to keep her alive. Only the patient can decide what is extraordinary, however, so the surgeon asked her, "If your heart stops beating during the operation, would you like me to start it again?" To which my friend replied, "Well, if it wouldn't be too much trouble, that would be nice."

These isolated acts of bravery are the steel rods on the construction site of your spiritual life. They provide the infrastructure upon which the temple of your faith is being built.

Your Curiosity Can Lessen Your Doubt

Thomas was also curious. Once when Jesus was speaking cryptically of life after death and the disciples did not understand him, Thomas alone had the courage to speak up. "Lord," he says, "we do *not* know where you are going; how *can* we know the way?" This paves the way for Jesus' great assertion: "I am the way, and the truth, and the life" (Jn 14:5-6, emphasis added).

It is with our questions as well as our acts of courage that the temple of belief is being built. Every question is another steel rod in its construction. Thomas doesn't understand, so he asks. What is the meaning of my life? Is there life beyond death?

"Those who wish to succeed must ask the right preliminary questions," Aristotle wrote. "I have no particular talent," Einstein said. "I am merely extremely inquisitive." He advised, "Never lose a holy curiosity."

Your History with Jesus Can Lessen Your Doubt

Thomas also had a history with Jesus. He had been with Jesus three years. As courageous and curious as he was, he probably would not have asked Jesus tough questions without this history.

So often we have doubts about our hearing a call when our history with Jesus, preparing us for a call, goes all the way back to childhood. Someone told me how he carries an image of Jesus that sustains him in tough times. It is an image from Sunday school of Jesus with his arms outstretched on the cross, and my friend stretched out his own arms as he said it.

Thomas found himself keeping his history with Jesus going. He kept asking his questions, making his bold moves. He experienced Jesus day and night. "It's like being in love," a man said to me once, describing his relationship to Christ. "You can't get the other person out of your mind. The image of the other person is constantly before you."

Such images of Christ are particularly needed these days, as two-thirds of the wars currently raging, according to the *New York Times,* are in the name of religion. Some of them even have different images of the same Christ on the two opposing sides.

Surely we need an image of Christ to do something about the death rate in our own country, which is three times higher for poor people than for the nonpoor. With the image of Christ constantly before her, Mother Teresa did something about the death rate in her adopted country of India. She herself is an image reminding us of the image of Christ.

Your Absence from Church May Be What You Need

The next time we meet Thomas he is away from the group. After appearing to Mary Magdalene, Jesus appears to the disciples, but Thomas is not among them. We have no idea where he was. Perhaps he had gone home. Perhaps he was attending to business. Perhaps he was looking for Jesus. Perhaps he was deep in his own private grief. All we know is that he was not there when Jesus was.

Your experience may parallel Thomas's. You have a history with Jesus, to be sure, but there are long periods when you may have been absent from the group, the other disciples, the church. Then, for example, your first child came, and you were mysteriously called back. Or you suffered some reversal in life and found yourself returning.

In story after story in the Bible, there is a time when the person of faith is away from the faith group, for whatever reason. Paul goes to Arabia before he begins his ministry. Jesus goes to the wilderness before he begins his. Moses runs from his people in flight for his life. "Fair seed time had my soul," Walt Whitman wrote. The experience of being away, far from condemning us to isolation from Christ, may be the very thing that brings us close.

Your Return to the Church May Be What You Need

Then the other disciples tell Thomas about the risen Jesus, and he utters the famous sentence, "Unless I see in his hands the print of the nails, and place my finger in the mark of the nails, and place my hand in his side, I will not believe" (Jn 20:25). Such a statement is completely in character for the bold asker of questions who has had a long history with Jesus, and it is tremendously reassuring to all who have histories similar to his.

Of particular importance is that, eight days later, Thomas felt called to return to the group. In only three instances—that of Mary Magdalene, Peter and Paul—is the resurrected Jesus recognized solo. And in both Mary's and Peter's cases, they, like Thomas, had been strong members of the group before Jesus appeared to them. This is powerful evidence for the importance of the church in helping us say, "My Lord and my God!"

Indeed, it was the church, the men and women who had been with Jesus those three years, that had nurtured Thomas all along. It was the church that had benefited from his bravery and curiosity and long history with the rest of them. We bring who we are to the church, but we receive as much as we give.

He had been away, but now he felt called back. There was something about those people and Jesus that drew him back. And it was in the coming back that he was able to say, "My Lord and my God!" John does not even record that he had to touch Jesus to believe. His past bravery, curiosity, history, leaving and returning had brought him to the point of recognition of Jesus as the Messiah. In other words, just being himself was enough for Thomas, and that, for all of us, should be immensely encouraging.

14

CALLS COME IN HUMILITY

Mary

L ife can take unexpected turns. You are on a certain career path when suddenly you find yourself off on another. You are interested in a particular college but get turned down; or, expecting to be rejected, you are surprised to find you are accepted. You hoped for a perfect child, but your child is born with a birth defect; or, you were afraid your child would be born with a birth defect, but your child appears to be perfect.

If you want to hear God calling, look at the turns life takes and how you are humbled by them. Mary wasn't even married, and suddenly she was expecting a child.

Your Call Is All Grace
"He who is mighty," Mary says, "has done great things for me" (Lk 1:49). It was a turn of momentous proportions. It was all God and no Mary. She had done nothing. She had not even participated in her child's conception. The Virgin Birth is a perfect symbol of passivity, of all grace and no will.

"Holy is his name," Mary continues. We feel we have entered another dimension when we are humbled by a turn life takes. "Midway life's journey," Dante wrote, "I was made aware / That I had strayed into a dark forest, / And the right path appeared not anywhere." It was a turning point for him, even though he did not know which way to turn, and in the turning point lay the holiness with its immense creativity, not only for him but for Mary and, potentially, for us.

"Put off your shoes from your feet," Moses hears God say, "for the place on which you are standing is holy ground" (Ex 3:5). It came at a turning point in Moses' life as crucial to him as Mary's was to her. And, as with Mary, it came when he was simply going about his everyday life.

"His mercy is on those who fear him," Mary says (Lk 1:50). The holy is in the fear Mary feels at her listening point. "Mercy" was the opposite of might. God is merciful as well as mighty, loving as well as judging.

The two aspects of the divine personality are in constant dialectic in the Bible. But when a choice has to be made, it is always made surprisingly—in favor of mercy. Unconditional love, as we have seen, is the supreme message of the Judeo-Christian tradition. That is why God is always forgiving Israel, no matter how many times Israel tries to control life's turning points.

God Keeps Calling

God keeps calling no matter how often the call is not heard. Eventually, a turning point will be of such momentous proportions that the call *will* be heard, or there will have been a sufficiency of turning points so that even a minuscule turning point will be enough for the call to be heard.

If we control our turning points rather than find ourselves humbled before them, if we control the direction we will take when the events of life bring us to a turning point, then we will invariably miss our listening point. What makes it a listening point and not just another of life's turning points is the holiness factor. We feel it in our helplessness and total passivity.

Mary calls herself "the handmaid of the Lord" (Lk 1:38). The word *handmaid* is a genteel translation of the Greek word *slave*. A slave had no rights, was completely helpless and totally passive in the hands of the owner.

The first Christians, as we saw in the call of Philemon, called themselves slaves. "Paul, a slave of Jesus Christ" (Rom 1:1). "Paul and Timothy, slaves of Christ Jesus" (Phil 1:1). "James, a slave of God" (Jas 1:1). "Simon

Peter, a slave and apostle of Jesus Christ" (2 Pet 1:1). "Jude, a slave of Jesus Christ" (Jude 1:1). In English Bibles the translation is almost always "servant," but the point is the same. These Christians felt the same way Mary did. They had no will of their own. "It is no longer I who live," Paul writes, "but Christ who lives in me" (Gal 2:20). "This is how one should regard us," he says, "as slaves of Christ" (1 Cor 4:1).

Our helplessness at a turning point is our first hint of God. If we are not helpless, if we know which way to turn in the forest, that may work for even the majority of turning points in life. But at the decisive turning points we need help. Feeling the need for help is how the holy appears. "Man must altogether despair of himself," Luther said, "in order to be made capable of receiving Christ's grace."

Mary is "greatly troubled," but the angel says to her, "Do not be afraid" (Lk 1:29-30). Troubled and afraid, she is helpless before what is happening to her.

Your Call Enables You to Do the Impossible

At this point Mary finds herself doing something she could not possibly have done on her own. You know it's a call, we have found, if you find yourself doing the impossible. "With God," the angel tells her, "nothing will be impossible" (Lk 1:37).

What she finds herself doing is not something she would have willed, nor is it something she would have done had she been in control of her turning point. That is what makes it a listening point. She finds herself composing a poem of unparalleled beauty and power, what one commentator has called "the most revolutionary document in the world."[1] Many remember that Mary sang the Magnificat, "My soul magnifies," but few remember the words.

There is, of course, some question whether the Magnificat is original with Mary. But even if the words were put into her mouth by Luke or composed by other early Christians, the same creativity as Dante's must have been stimulated in them by their listening points. The one who is chosen to speak the holy words does not matter. What matters is the holy words.

In this song, Mary speaks of three revolutions. First, she describes a moral revolution, a moral turning point. "He has scattered the proud in the imagination of their hearts" (Lk 1:51). The proud will be humbled. It is a complete reversal of values. Normally, the proud are exalted. "All existing order will be turned upside down," writes a commentator. "All present standards of measurement will be reversed."[2]

Second, she describes a political revolution. "He has put down the mighty from their thrones" (1:52). The Hebrew people were under the rule of Rome and wanted nothing so much as their independence.

Third, she describes an economic revolution. "He has filled the hungry with good things, and the rich he has sent empty away" (1:53). The humble will be exalted, the weak will be empowered, the poor will be enriched. That is the Christian revolution. But how will it be accomplished? Through the suffering and death of Mary's child.

You Become a Handmaid
How can this be, Mary asks, that she should have a child without a husband (Lk 1:34)? We ask the same question of the Christian revolution. How can it be? It can only be as we find ourselves becoming humble handmaids of the Lord. "Let it be to me according to your word," she says (1:38). She is the acme of humility.

The Greeks hated the word *humble*. They only used it disparagingly.[3] Mary says God "has regarded the low estate of his handmaiden" (1:48). But that would never do for the Greeks. "How can a man be happy," Plato wrote, "who is the servant of anything?"[4]

There was no place for kneeling in the Greek religion because kneeling was the attitude of a slave before a master. Of course, that was precisely the attitude the early Christians adopted; they did so because it was in their tradition. Abraham was called God's servant (Ps 105:42). So, for example, were Jacob (Is 48:20), Joshua (Judg 2:8), David (Ps 89:3) and the Suffering Servant (Is 53:11).

The trouble the Greeks had with the image of the slave was that it took away the power of choice. The number one virtue for the Greek was freedom.[5] For the Christian it was obedience. There is a conflict in us between freedom and obedience, queen and handmaid, Greek and Christian, outer and inner self.

That conflict is won by obedience, at least for a while, when the unexpected turns of life bring us to a listening point. These turns are there for a reason, to humble us to the point where, at last, we can hear the call of God.

15

CALLS COME IN HOSPITALITY

Cleopas

H*ave you ever wished for an experience in which everything came* together and you felt you were on top of the world? You would be able to handle anything, free to live in the present, free to be spontaneous and joyful. Such an experience is available to you when you hear the call of the risen Christ. The story of two people who did is instructive because it shows how you can too.

A man named Cleopas is trudging home with a companion after the crucifixion of Jesus. They are talking about what happened when Jesus, unrecognized, draws near and walks along with them. He asks them to tell him what they are discussing. They do so and then add how they had hoped that Jesus would be the Messiah.

At this point, Jesus explains to them the messianic passages in the Bible, and eventually they arrive at the village that is their destination. Cleopas and his companion invite Jesus to stay with them, and as he blesses and breaks the bread, they recognize him.

Your Call Comes When There Are Two of You
There were two of them, Cleopas and his companion. The companion

could have been his wife or a friend. We will never know. What matters is that they were together. In all the resurrection stories, there are only three instances of Jesus appearing to people who were alone.

"Where two or three are gathered in my name," Jesus said, "there am I in the midst of them" (Mt 18:20). There is something about being with someone else that facilitates the appearance of Christ. It can be a spouse, a child, a sibling, a friend, or companions in a discipleship group or a church.

There is an old story about a man having coffee before the fire with his friend, the famed evangelist Dwight L. Moody. "You know, Dwight," the man said, "I've always thought I could be a perfectly good Christian without being a member of a church." Moody said nothing but reached forward to the fireplace with the tongs and pulled out a coal and held it in the air. Gradually it died.

When Jesus said, "Where two or three are gathered in my name, there am I," he was saying something fundamental about the Christian experience, that is, about hearing the call of the risen Christ. We need each other.

I heard the call of the risen Christ in that small group of Christians in college. I will never forget the feeling of being on top of the world, free, spontaneous, joyful. All we were doing was reading the Bible together, sharing experiences and praying. But that was enough. In the togetherness, it was enough.

Your Call Comes When You Have a Relationship with Jesus

Cleopas and his companion already had a relationship with Jesus. They were part of the group that had been with him. You may already have a relationship with Christ. It may be tenuous, of course. You may not have been in church for years and may never have been in a small group. Or you may have been a strong church member all your life. It doesn't matter. All that matters is that you have some relationship to Jesus. According to this story, you will be able to hear Jesus' call.

But we must enter the usual caveat in our retelling of a Bible story. This was their story. It does not have to be ours. Just because it happened this way for Cleopas and his companion does not mean it will happen this way for us. The Bible's stories, we have discovered, are descriptive rather then prescriptive, since we cannot limit the Holy Spirit to any one way of acting. However, the stories suggest that if certain Bible people heard a call in a certain way, it is entirely possible that we could hear a call in a similar way.

Your Call Comes When You Are Having a Religious Conversation

Cleopas and his companion were engaged in a religious conversation. They were "talking with each other about all these things that had happened," namely, the events of the last few days surrounding Jesus' arrest and execution (Lk 24:14).

It is immensely heartening to hear about the number of religious conversations taking place in colleges. Students are flocking to religion courses. But you don't have to take a course to talk religiously. Any time you ask a question about ultimate meaning you are talking religiously. Any time you ask where you go when you die, or whether another dimension actually exists, you are talking religiously.

It is after a conversation about that other dimension of life—namely, the theological beyond the psychological, sociological and ecological— that the risen Christ appears. In other words, the religious conversation has sensitized the two of them to the possibility of the risen Christ's appearing. The more you find yourself talking religiously, either broadly or narrowly defined, the readier you will be for the incognito Christ to appear.

Your Call Comes When You Are Expressing Your Feelings Honestly

Cleopas and the other person are dejected. "And they stood still, looking sad" (Lk 24:17). Their conversation has led to feelings of hopelessness and loss: "We had hoped that he was the one to redeem Israel," but since he had been crucified as a common criminal, obviously he wasn't (24:21).

Be honest about your feelings about Christ. He may be completely unimportant to you. Say so in your religious conversations. I love the honesty of young people talking about Christ. If they don't understand something, they say so. If they don't believe something, they say so. That is what a religious conversation is all about, and if it leads to feelings of dejection, that's all right. Honesty about thinking and feeling is all the risen Christ asks.

Your Call Comes When You Turn to the Bible

Jesus walked along with Cleopas and his companion and "interpreted to them in all the scriptures the things concerning himself" (Lk 24:27).

Thomas Merton, the famed Trappist monk, became a Catholic because the religious instruction he received had been so important to him. In the priesthood of all believers, we are all instructors for each other, since it is as we study the Bible together that the inner meaning of the Scriptures can be revealed and their relevance become clear.

My small-group experience in college, talking religiously with friends every week and reading the Bible together, was so helpful to me in experiencing the risen Christ that, often since, I have participated in one or another small group. In one such group, we would take a few verses each week, read them aloud, and then talk about how they related to our lives.

But why should we read the Bible. Because we can't not read it. We are drawn to it out of our need for a more abundant life. We have a feeling that the Bible can free us from guilt that chains us to the past and from worry that chains us to the future. We will be free at last to live in the present, to be spontaneous, joyful, happy.

Your Call Comes When You Show Hospitality

"Stay with us," they say to the stranger, Jesus, "for it is toward evening and the day is now far spent" (Lk 24:29). They show hospitality to a stranger. This simple act, on top of everything that has gone before it, is of such profound importance that it will reveal the risen Christ. Jesus can appear when we find ourselves doing something for someone else.

Their being together, their prior relationship with Jesus, their religious talk, their dejection, their study of the Bible—all bring them to this moment. Would they have asked the stranger to stay with them if the other things had not happened first? Possibly, but all we have to go on is what actually happened. They were moved to extend their invitation because of what had gone before.

What can we do for the strangers in our midst, above and beyond what we are already doing through our taxes? Think of the homeless in your city. Think of the 10 percent of the country below the poverty line. Think of the other 10 percent just above the poverty line. Think of the 15 percent who have no health insurance.

Cleopas and his companion invite Jesus in and they eat together. It is during the meal that they recognize him. "He took the bread and blessed, and broke it, and gave it to them. And their eyes were opened and they recognized him" (Lk 24:30-31). It reads like a communion service, perhaps designedly so. In the communion, we can often hear the call of the risen Christ most clearly.

Your Call Is Obeyed When You Find Yourself Telling About Christ

Soon after Jesus vanishes from their sight they tell their friends about him. Spontaneous and joyful, they leave the table and hurry back to Jerusalem, and there "they told what had happened on the road" (24:35).

When the risen Christ calls, you are moved to tell people about it. And you will—if you have been honest about your feelings, talked about ultimate matters, read up on them, discussed them with others, and then found yourself doing something for somebody else.

Part IV

CALLS ARE HEARD IN
NEGATIVE EMOTIONAL
EXPERIENCES

16

CALLS COME IN ANGUISH

Hannah

There are no easy answers when you are in emotional pain, but there is at least one difficult answer if it can break through—the answer of the call of God. Normally, the call of God is the farthest thing from our thoughts, but when we are in profound pain we may find ourselves in touch with God as never before.

God May Be Nearest When You Think God Is Farthest

Take, for instance, the story of Hannah (1 Sam 1—2). She is in anguish over her inability to have a child: "She was deeply distressed," the Bible reports (1:10). She "wept and would not eat" (1:7). She "wept bitterly" (1:10). "I am a woman sorely troubled," she says (1:15).

When we are sorely troubled the God who appears farthest may be nearest. "The stars shine out," Carlyle observed, "as soon as it is dark enough." But how do we know God is near?

There are four ways of knowing: the rational, in which we form concepts; the empirical, in which we make observations; the intuitional, in which we have hunches; and the revelational, in which we actually experience God.

Hannah's experience of the call of God begins, as most such experiences begin, in the empirical, with something happening to her in her everyday life—in her case the pain of her inability to conceive. One can argue, of course, that this is "foxhole religion," but if God can't be in the foxholes of life, then where?

You Find Yourself Acting on a Hunch

Suddenly Hannah finds herself acting on a hunch. She gets up from the table because she can't eat and goes to the temple—not the office, not the school, but the temple. Something draws her—a hunch that it will be here, if anywhere, that she will hear God's call.

I have sat with numerous people who were drawn to the temple in profound emotional pain. They found themselves drawn to a place devoted to the four ways of knowing. They were acting on a hunch that it was here that they could experience God, which would be the only experience strong enough to sustain them in their pain.

One might think that a temple would be devoted only to the fourth way of knowing, revelation, but so often we do not get the flash of revelation until we have gone through experience, reason and hunch. We want the flash without the hunch, or we want the hunch without the need, or we want the need without the thought. But short-circuiting the process is rarely the way to hear the call of God.

Once I was with a man who told me about his son, who had been sorely troubled about his career as a journalist. He had been out on a story in Texas when he stopped to pick up a hitchhiker. With the towns in that part of Texas far apart, the next two hours became two of the most remarkable of his life.

The hitchhiker had been released recently from prison and, among other things, was full of questions about God. The two of them found themselves in a theological discussion such as my friend's son had never had. They were engaged in the rational way of knowing.

But the driver's rationality, his feeling troubled about his career and his acting on his hunch to pick up the hitchhiker somehow all combined to turn his pickup truck into a temple. He described it to his father: "The whole front of the cab was on fire!" He said further that he was actually experiencing God. Concept, percept, hunch and flash had done their work. Subsequently, he felt called to leave journalism, go to seminary, and is now pastor of a Presbyterian church.

What the temple does—and the temple could be, as the hitchhiker story illustrates, anywhere—is help us sort out our thoughts, think through our experiences, act on our hunches and receive revelation. This does not always happen, of course, but it happens often enough to make the temple, the church, a place to go when we are sorely troubled, and it happens often enough for us to be open to its happening anywhere, where any place could be our listening place.

You Find Yourself Praying

Hannah finds herself feeling her feeling. She doesn't run from it through alcohol or work. Then she finds herself acting on a hunch rather than shrugging it off. Next, she finds herself praying, but not an ordinary prayer. "She was deeply distressed and prayed to the LORD, and wept bitterly" (1 Sam 1:10). "Hannah was speaking in her heart," the Bible says (1:13).

She was taking her intuitive action all the way. It not only took her away from the dinner table, it found her straining every ounce of will and intellect and emotion to hear God speak. That is what the Bible means when it says Hannah was "speaking in her heart."

"The heart has its reasons," Pascal said, "which reason does not know." He was the most brilliant mathematician and philosopher of his time, when one day he was thrown from his carriage and almost killed. The experience made a difference in how he thought about things. The man who all his life had been devoted to the first way of knowing, the rational, suddenly found himself in the worst experience of his life and in desperate need of help.

He began to act on a hunch about God, and on November 23, 1654, he got his flash. "FIRE," he wrote in capital letters. "God of Abraham, God of Isaac, God of Jacob, not of the philosophers and scholars. Certitude, certitude, feeling, joy, peace. God of Jesus Christ . . . Joy, joy, joy, tears of joy. I have been separated from him. . . . Jesus Christ, Jesus Christ. I have been separated from him; I have fled him, renounced him, crucified him. Let me never be separated from him. . . Total submission to Jesus Christ."

"I have been pouring out my soul before the LORD," Hannah says (1 Sam 1:15). "I have been speaking out of my great anxiety and vexation" (1:16). She holds nothing back. "Whatever you ask in prayer," Jesus said, "believe that you have received it, and it will be yours" (Mk 11:24). "If you ask anything in my name, I will do it" (Jn 14:14).

Someone Helps You Hear God's Call

When you are in deep emotional pain you can hear God's call if you find yourself being honest about your feelings and acting on your intuitive hunches about yourself and about God—and if you find yourself being helped by someone.

Someone else is with Hannah. He had been there all along while she was praying. Eli, the temple priest, had watched her praying and thought she was drunk because while she prayed, "only her lips moved, and her voice was not heard" (1 Sam 1:13). The normal practice was to pray out loud.

Eli could give her what the events of her life had brought her to the temple for—a word from God. "Go in peace," he says, "and the God of Israel grant your petition which you have made" (1:17).

Often we need someone else to help us hear God call. A young man was leaving church one Sunday after the painful loss of a relationship with a woman. His pastor, who knew of his loss, said to him at the door, "Remember, you *will* be healed. That is the gospel."

The reminder that God is calling, no matter how painful our situation, often comes through someone else. David had Nathan to remind him in the pain of his adultery. Naomi had Ruth to remind her in the pain of their departure from Ruth's homeland. Paul had Ananias in the pain of losing his sight at his conversion. It happens so often in the Bible that there must be something to it.

A tourist visited the sequoias in California. He was astonished when the guide said they did not have deep roots. "But they must have," the tourist said, "or the wind would blow them over." "You'd think so," the guide replied, "but you will notice how they always grow in groves, and when the wind comes they stay standing because their roots intertwine and give each other strength."

You Discover That God Remembers You

After Eli's revelation that God would grant her petition, Hannah feels better. She "went her way and ate, and her countenance was no longer sad" (1 Sam 1:18). Often you know it was a good prayer if you feel better after it. She goes back to her meal. The calm light of reason returns.

Now is the time for thinking things through. Our pain begins to come into focus after the initial upheaval and after we have "taken it to the Lord in prayer." We have an idea of God after we have a hunch for God, a hunch that comes in turn after some deep feeling, such as longing for a child, which is so deep it has driven us to our knees and to other people.

Hannah and her husband rise early the next morning. They go back to the temple, they return home, they make love. That's all there is, just the ordinary stuff of life, but somehow extraordinary because, as the Bible says, "The LORD remembered her" (1:19).

That's what we are after in our distress. We just want to know God remembers us. That will be call enough. And perhaps, in the calm light of reason, after our own huge emotion, fervent prayers and outside help, we can see that God was there all along. Maybe that's what revelation is—among other things—the sudden seeing, as Pascal saw and the young man in the pickup saw, that God was there all along—the sudden knowing that we are remembered.

17

CALLS COME IN DISCOURAGEMENT
Matthew

The Greek word for sin *in the New Testament means "to miss the mark."* Matthew had missed the mark, badly. He had failed to measure up to his expectations for himself, let alone God's expectations, and he was discouraged. Remarkably, it was his very failure to measure up that, over time, brought him to a listening point. If there was hope for him, surely there can be hope for us.

You Feel You Have Wasted Your Life

Matthew was considered a particularly egregious sinner, since he was a tax collector and tax collectors were classed with thieves and murderers. Why? Because they worked for the occupation army and because they could charge whatever they felt the traffic would bear.

A tax collector could keep anything he collected above what Rome wanted. Nobody, of course, had any idea what Rome wanted since there were no newspapers and the taxes were never posted. To make matters worse, tax collectors could be bribed by the wealthy so they would not have to pay any taxes at all.

The taxes in Jesus' time were particularly onerous. They were 10 percent on your grain, 20 percent on your wine, 1 percent on your income, 2.5 percent to 12.5 percent on your imports and exports. There was a poll tax, a tollway tax, a bridge tax, a shopping mall tax, a town tax, a harbor tax, a pack animal tax, an axle tax, a wheel tax and, on top of all that, a sales tax.[1] It is often suggested that people could afford to tithe in Jesus' day because they weren't as heavily taxed as we are. Nothing could be further from the truth.

Matthew was sitting at a tollbooth down by the harbor, ready to slap an export tax on anything that left town. Doubtless he was alone. Tax collectors were such pariahs that they were not allowed in the synagogues and could not bear witness in the courts.[2] It is entirely possible that, reflecting alone in his booth, Matthew concluded that he was wasting his life.

You too might be reaching the same conclusion. Your sin may not be as obvious as his, but when you consider all you have done that you ought not to have done, as the prayer goes, and all you have not done that you ought to have done, there would appear to be fertile ground indeed for your own listening points.

A Substitute Jesus Walks into Your Life

Matthew probably knew Jesus. His listening point appears to have been in Capernaum, a port town on the Sea of Galilee. It is a small town, and Jesus was often there. There was plenty of opportunity for them to meet.

Most of Western civilization knows about Jesus, so readers of this book will have as casual an acquaintance with him as Matthew had. This means that we can be called as he was—if, that is, we have someone standing in for Jesus to do the calling. We need someone to say, at the right moment in our sinfulness, "Follow Jesus."

Jesus sees Matthew sitting in his tax office and says simply, "Follow me" (Lk 5:27). The timing is perfect; Matthew is ready. He has become sufficiently discouraged with the life he is leading. He is at a listening point.

When being wide of the mark bothers you enough, and when someone else offers you a better way with Jesus, you too could be at a listening point. Note that it takes both the bothering and the offering. The one has to be sufficient for the other to be effective. Many know about Jesus but have never been challenged by a proxy for Jesus. By the same token, many challenged by a proxy may have been challenged too soon. The challenge doesn't take. It isn't a listening point. They aren't discouraged enough with how they are living their lives.

Your Joy Knows No Bounds

At this point an unusual thing happens. Matthew throws a dinner party for Jesus. "And [Matthew] made him a great feast in his house; and there was a large company of tax collectors and others sitting at table with them" (Lk 5:29).

The appropriate response to a listening point is joy. Remember, you know it's a call if you experience love, joy and peace. Matthew celebrates. As an order of service for communion reads: "This is the joyful feast of the people of God." The communion is the church's weekly dinner party with Jesus, a celebration of the resurrection.

Mother Teresa was called at the age of eighteen to be a missionary to India. "How can I be sure?" she asked her priest in Skopje, Macedonia. "Through your joy," he replied.

Joy is at the heart of the Christian life. A joyless Christian is a contradiction in terms. "His disciples should look more redeemed," Nietzsche said. Matthew had it exactly right. The odious one, the ostracized one, the quisling knows exactly how to behave once he reaches a listening point. He celebrates.

And there, on the fringes, are the Pharisees, doing what Pharisees do best—criticizing: "Why do you eat and drink with tax collectors and sinners?" they ask the disciples (Lk 5:30). Pharisees would never dine with tax collectors and sinners. All such people would be beneath them. Their self-righteousness throws Matthew's joy into even bolder relief.

You Find Yourself Going Out to Those Who Need You

Discouraged, challenged, joyful—there is a final element to Matthew's listening point. It is to go out to those who need him in response to Jesus' call. "I desire mercy," Jesus explains to the Pharisees, "and not sacrifice" (Mt 9:13). Life is not a matter of ritual correctness, he tells them. It is a matter of going out to fellow sinners who need us.

Matthew goes out. He becomes one of the twelve disciples, and a number of scholars say he wrote the book that bears his name, a book in which are recorded countless acts of mercy.

To whom are you feeling called to be merciful? A friend? Family member? Homeless person? Refugee?

I had a twenty-seven-year-old friend who developed a particularly virulent form of cancer. Two weeks before her death she got into her wheelchair at the hospital to see me off at the elevator. There, waiting for the elevator, was an old woman sitting on a bench and looking confused.

"Are you lost?" my young friend asked. "Can I help you?"

It was an act of mercy by one for whom such acts were about to end. I was stunned by its ingenuousness.

A call is not a call unless it eventuates in acts of mercy. Discouraged, challenged, joyful, you find yourself, a redeemed sinner, reaching out to those in need. And you know it isn't you doing the reaching but Christ reaching through you. "Apart from me," Jesus said, "you can do nothing" (Jn 15:5). Every act of mercy becomes a witness to Christ.

18

CALLS COME IN FLIGHT
Moses

A *friend was telling me about all the things she wanted to do in her life* but how she had not really done any of them except one big one —being the mother of three children. That was fine, of course, except there were all these other things she had not gotten around to yet, and now, with time running out, she was afraid she never would.

You Are Running from Something
Like my friend, Moses was running from something. He had just killed a man and was in flight for his life. He had taken the law into his own hands and murdered an Egyptian who was beating a Hebrew slave. He had hoped it would go unnoticed, but apparently it had not. "Then Moses was afraid," the Bible says, and he fled (Ex 2:14-15).

It was a false start on his adult life. His instincts were good in taking up the cause of an oppressed people. But his impetuosity was less good, and it did him in. Now he was reaping the consequences of his fear, just as my friend was reaping the consequences of hers.

My friend was in hiding from herself because of fear—fear of change, fear of failure, fear of the unknown. Such fear is insidious, working its way into every aspect of our personalities.

Ironically, my friend has not passed on her fear to her children. They are high achievers, each having made a fine start in life, with one garnering a B.A. and two M.A.s in five years, and the others in highly paid professions. Two are full-time mothers with no regrets, and the third is successfully combining job and home.

You Are Sidetracked

Moses in flight turns out to be Moses on a detour from the main track of his life. He marries and settles down in Midian, far from Egypt, where he becomes executive vice-president of his father-in-law's sheep business. He has a comfortable home, a wife and child, retirement assured, social security and a warm climate. What more could anyone ask?

A lot more. When we are hiding because we are afraid, we are likely to trick ourselves into believing we are all we could and should be when we aren't. Our very comfort keeps us from dealing with our fear. My friend had been in hiding for twenty years, ever since her last child had left home. The security of having a well-paid husband had prevented her from becoming all she was meant to be. It had kept her waiting on a sidetrack and off the main track of her life.

Our comfort, however, does not mean that we cannot hear God's call. Indeed, as in the case of Moses, our comfort is the very thing preparing us to hear the call. Moses is afraid. He goes into hiding. He stays in hiding because it is comfortable. Little does he know that he is about to be rocketed out of hiding and sent directly back into the very place he had fled so fearfully. In the midst of his comfort, the bush is about to burn.

Out of her comfort, in which she was hiding from her fear of change, my friend started talking to me at a dinner party with eight of us seated around a table. The very fact that she was sharing so intimately in such a public setting indicated that her comfort was beginning to become uncomfortable. The happenstance that I was seated next to her somehow gave her a hint of something more to life than she was currently experiencing. Otherwise she would not have opened up to me.

The bush could never have burned for Moses if he had not been afraid and fled, married and settled down and had a child, and gone into business. The bush would never be able to burn for my friend if she had not married and settled down and had three children and been afraid of who she might become and fled from her fear into a comfortable life.

In other words, it has to be the way it has to be for each of us to hear God's call. If fear and flight work for you the way they worked for Moses, fine. If not, equally fine. One or another of the Bible's calls will more closely fit your particular life.

Something Catches Your Attention

Moses is afraid and because of his fear becomes sidetracked. Suddenly, he is to be sent back into his fear because the call comes. A bush bursts into flame and catches his attention. Nothing unusual at first; bushes do burn. But this one keeps burning.

There has to be a sign to indicate that we are at a listening point, at least according to the Moses story. Something has to catch our attention. You know it may be a call when something normally insignificant, like a bush, suddenly becomes significant. A dinner party companion, normally insignificant, could suddenly burst into significance as you find yourself confiding in him or her.

For Moses, it was a flame that signaled God; for Amos, a plumb line; for Isaiah, a worship service. Something that would not normally catch our attention catches it. It is inexplicable but incomparably full of grace, pregnant with God.

The signal that it is God calling is not something we devise. It is completely external to us. It could be a phone call. It could be a chance meeting at a class reunion. It could be a communion wafer. It could be something a child or spouse says. Something ordinary suddenly becomes extraordinary.

But it didn't happen until now. Moses had to have all that fear and flight and comfort beforehand. The bush didn't burn the day he left Egypt. It may not have burned that night at the dinner party for my friend. Only time will tell. There may have to be more dinner parties, more intimate conversations. Whatever has to happen will.

How long do we have to wait for a sign? Who knows? It takes whatever it takes to hear a call. Something may trigger the thought that you have been afraid long enough, or the feeling that what you are doing may be all right but just isn't you. Something may lead you to notice how you are taking out your unease on your kids, or eating too much or sleeping too little, or how impatient, irascible and petulant you have become. Your burning bush could be your own child, whom you discover to your horror you have just slapped.

You Find Yourself on the Main Track of Your Life

Moses was converted. The word comes from the root for "turn around." Moses had to be spun around, sent off in a new direction, the one in which he would be true to himself at last.

Moses was a leader, with a fine sense of justice. That was why he had killed the Egyptian in the first place. It was why he had tried to intervene in a dispute between two slaves and why he had championed the cause of some women at a well who were being bullied by a gang of shepherds (Ex 2:15-20).

God is the power in your life enabling you to be the person you were meant to be. Suddenly, your bush will burn and you will find yourself doing whatever it is that is most you. Perhaps it will be what you enjoyed most as a youth, what you loved to do, what you lost yourself doing, what you liked yourself for doing—with no fear or petulance, no sleeplessness or gluttony, no impatience or irascibility.

But you may arrive at your listening point only after being far from it in fear and off the main track of your life for years. And that's all right. If that kind of process can produce the new Moses, it can also produce the new you.

And what of my dinner party friend? Every time she finds herself talking about her fear of change, she will be that much closer to her burning bush.

19

CALLS COME IN DESPAIR

Elijah

Who of us, at one time or another, has not lost hope? You may have lost your job or even your parent, spouse, or child. Or you may feel hopeless about your job or about one of your children. Perhaps you even despair of life itself. "How can I possibly hear the call of God," we ask, "in the depths of despair?"

Of What Do You Despair?
Elijah of Tishbe in Gilead had lost hope. Having just defeated the 450 prophets of Baal in the celebrated contest on Mt. Carmel, he was now fleeing for his life. In one stunning blow, he had lost his country, his family and his job. With everything gone, he had also lost, perhaps inevitably, his self-image and his hope. "O LORD," he says under a broom tree, "take away my life" (1 Kings 19:4).

At that moment, "an angel touched him" (19:5). It seems wildly improbable, but there it is. The point of despair becomes the point of hope. When you hit rock bottom, you hit rock. Not always, of course, but it can happen, and happen often enough not only to get into the Bible but also to remind us that our point of despair can become a listening point, as it became for Elijah, who soon hears the "still small voice" (19:12).

Perhaps a key to the angel's arrival was Elijah's acknowledgment of his despair. We often deny our negative feelings, like anger, fear, frustration and guilt. We either bury them or project them. This can lead to cancer on the one hand and hurt feelings on the other. One of our greatest challenges is to integrate the dark side of who we are. If we fail to do so, we can easily disintegrate.

In spite of the acknowledgment of his despair, Elijah was in danger of disintegrating. "He was afraid, and he arose and went for his life" (19:3). His despair led him to a broom tree after which, he continued another forty days in flight to a cave in a mountain.

Of what are you afraid in your despair? What we fear the most may bring God the most. At least it has that potential, according to the story of Elijah. As we have seen, fear is the negative root emotion, love the positive. The Bible puts the two together in its root statement, the Shema Israel: "Hear, O Israel" (Deut 6:4). "That you may fear the LORD your God. . . . And you shall love the LORD your God with all your heart" (6:2, 5).

You Find Yourself Accepting Yourself

God is what enables us to accept our negative as well as positive emotions. As theologian Paul Tillich put it, "We experience moments in which we accept ourselves, because we feel that we have been accepted by that which is greater than we. If only more such moments were given us! For it is such moments that make us love our life, that make us accept ourselves, not in our goodness and self-complacency, but in our certainty of the eternal meaning of our life."[1] Tillich is describing a listening point.

The love of God, explains a Bible expert, is never separated from the fear of God.[2] They are integrated in the godhead. You can never have the one without the other, a fact that is by no means always understood. That is why there have always been paradoxical aspects of God in the Bible and in other religions. God is both justice and mercy, Judge and Redeemer, fearsome and loving, and has both so-called masculine and feminine characteristics.

By the same token, there are both masculine and feminine aspects of each of us. Only one chromosome makes the difference between whether we are male or female. What happened to all the other chromosomes? They are still there.

So if you are a man, one key to your growth (which means in religious terms one key to your arrival at a listening point) is to find yourself in touch with your so-called feminine side, the part of you that is sensitive and deals with relationships and feelings. Is it any wonder that God speaks to the men we are looking at in the Bible through their emotions?

If you are a woman, one key to your growth, to your listening point, is to find yourself in touch with your so-called masculine side, the part that is rational and deals with logical constructs. Is it any wonder that God speaks to Deborah through her powerful leadership as a judge of Israel?

Logos and eros unite in these powerful moments of self-awareness. The logical, masculine self is at one with the relational, feminine self. It is in such unions, such "at-one-ments" that the still small voice is heard. It is these unions that produce our listening points. When such a union occurs under the momentum of time and events, that is when we say life has brought us to a listening point and we can at last hear God's call. The call will be to do the impossible thing we are asked to do at this point in life and will result in a radical change in our behavior.

Jesus Helps You Accept Your Negative Side

Jesus, we discover, is uniquely qualified, as the most balanced, most "together" person, to effect this at-one-ment through his atonement. His life becomes the agent of change for our lives. We are at one with ourselves because of him. Our outer and inner selves are fused as we find ourselves contemplating the perfect fusion of masculine and feminine in him.

Of all people, Jesus was the one capable of evoking his soul, and he was able to do so because of his being in constant touch with God the Father. As Elijah was touched by the angel, so was Jesus in his wilderness experience. "Angels came and ministered to him" (Mt 4:11). We too are similarly touched in our wilderness experiences of despair as we find ourselves put in touch with our opposite.

But the fusion of opposites in the self is not always available to us without suffering. That appears to be the wisdom of the atonement, first hinted in the story of the Hebrew people. The suffering of the Suffering Servant, Israel to Jews and Jesus to Christians, has the uncanny ability, as Isaiah knew, to fuse our opposites, to atone, to put us at one with ourselves, no longer a house divided, as Jesus said (Mk 3:25), but united in a uniquely powerful fusion.

When the negative and positive aspects of ourselves are integrated at a listening point, extraordinary energy is released and we get an Elijah who now can take on the entire religio-political establishment. As Elijah's feelings moved him, God the potential became God the actual. God spoke to him through his feelings, through his despair and his fear.

It is our emotions (from the root for "move out") that move the inmost self out so it is, at last, available. Mostly we keep hiding from it because we are afraid of its power over us, and we want to remain in control at all costs. But our emotions are precisely what we cannot control. They will out—if, that is, we find ourselves being true to them and not denying or projecting them. But we will only stop denying and projecting when enough events have accumulated to let the emotions through.

Accepting Your Negative Side Helps You Do the Impossible

When being and doing, inner and outer, are fused by huge emotion, that is when we find ourselves doing the impossible. Elijah, the sometime doer of phenomenal deeds—one man beating 450—finds himself united at his listening point, in his despair, to the ground of his being—God.

"What are you doing here, Elijah?" God asks sarcastically (1 Kings 19:13). It is the still small voice. It is also the last thing Elijah wants to hear. But that doesn't matter. It never does. Moses didn't want to hear about going back to Egypt. Paul didn't want to hear about loving the Christians he hated.

Elijah finds himself doing the opposite of what he wanted to do. He wanted to stay in the cave where it was safe. Instead, he finds the still small voice saying, "Go, return," where it was not safe, where he would have to do battle with yet another establishment, this one in Syria (19:15-18). After your being and doing have been fused, your first work is finding yourself doing what you never dreamed you would.

Deborah finds herself marshaling an army. Isaiah finds himself prophesying. Nicodemus finds himself standing up for Jesus. You know you are in touch with your inner self when you find yourself doing something you would never do on your own. That is why we say that you "find yourself" doing it.

That isn't me, you say, incredulous. You bet it's you. It is the lost part of you, your inner self, your soul, revealed at last by your listening point. It is the still small voice speaking through your voice and doing, through you, what you never dreamed you could.

20

CALLS COME IN FRUSTRATION

Peter

One of the greatest frustrations regarding a call is the speed with which it disappears. Our calls come in moments, and to have the moment vanish no sooner than it arrives can be frustrating in the extreme.

You Cannot Seem to Keep the Precious Moments of Life
Peter experienced this frustration on the Mount of Transfiguration. Jesus' position as the Son of God has just been confirmed by the appearance of Elijah and Moses, thus confirming, in effect, Peter's own call as a disciple of the Son. "This is my beloved Son," God says of Jesus, "listen to him" (Mk 9:7). Peter's response to the initial experience is to try to keep the moment by suggesting they make three booths in which to hold the three men (9:5).

It would seem to be in the nature of things that the most precious moments of life, including our listening points, are the most frustrating, because they cannot be kept.

Our daughter, her husband and child had been in town for a visit. We waved goodbye as they left. They rolled down their windows and waved vigorously back. I took out my handkerchief and waved it in an age-old gesture my father had used, and his father before him. They turned the corner, then came the tears.

I remember my mother standing in the driveway waving goodbye as I set off for college and graduate school and summer jobs. Then when I came home with my new family, there she would be, waving goodbye when we left. When we turned the corner, her tears began to flow. The precious moment of our time together was gone.

The last child goes to kindergarten, and it is quiet in the house. The last child goes to college, and it is quiet again. All your jokes to your friends about "a little peace and quiet for a change" cannot cover your loneliness. You go up to your child's room and muse, and there is a sadness. It seems only a moment that your child was with you, and now your child is gone.

Your child gets married, and you know your child will rarely again be coming home, and then not alone, and there is a wistfulness in that. Something has changed. Your family system has been altered, and what was, is no more. There may be tears for that at the wedding, for what used to be, for a beautiful time together, gone now forever. Gerald Manley Hopkins wrote:

> How to keep—is there any any, is there none such, nowhere
>   known some, bow or brooch or braid or brace, lace, latch or
>   catch or key to keep
> Back beauty, keep it, beauty, beauty, beauty, . . .
>   from vanishing away?[1]

Peter wanted to keep the moment. He wanted to keep the call, box it, freeze it, so there would be no more driveways, no more empty rooms upstairs. This moment was what life was all about. He was in the presence of God. He knew it by the deep emotion of fear he was feeling before the numinous appearance of the divine (Mk 9:6).

How do your keep your listening points? "Is there any any, is there none such, nowhere known some" booth? Is there something you could build? A temple? A church? Some architecture that would hold the moment forever? A picture to have beside you in the hospital while you wait for word from the surgeon?

How can we transfix the transfiguration? How can we keep God? How can we hold those moments of time when the other, in the most loving experiences of life, is transfigured before us? What can we build? What can we write? What can we paint or draw?

How can I keep you from growing up? How can I keep you in the same city? The same state? How can I keep you from dying? Peter had just stood in Jesus' way by demanding that he not go to Jerusalem and face certain death (Mk 8:31-33). How can I keep you forever? I will do anything to keep the moment of time that was your life and our life together.

Everything we do to keep life's precious moments is good, make no mistake. But the frustrating truth is that it goes only so far. We will write symphonies and poems and speeches and books. We will go back to class reunions and celebrate anniversaries and birthdays. We will put up stones in graveyards and keep our children's first-grade artwork until it mildews in our files.

But none of it seems to work. None of it seems to last. None of it seems to keep the precious moments of life that are sifting through our fingers. There is no booth of our construction that is big enough or strong enough or creative enough to preserve the lasting in the fleeting. "The only constant is change," Heraclitus said. "There is no enduring remembrance," the Bible says (Eccles 2:16). "Life ... passes like a shadow" (Eccles 6:12).

You Keep the Precious Moments of Life When You Love

But there is a way to keep the precious moments of life. The answer is in the transfiguration story. Jesus' "garments became glistening, intensely white, as no fuller on earth could bleach them" (Mk 9:3). Light was a symbol of the presence of God. God would be the only permanence. That was what Peter would learn.

God appears in those moments when the meaning of life is brought to light—in the driveway, the child's room, the wedding. The meaning of life is love, the first of the nine transformational marks of a call. When we find ourselves loving so much it brings tears to our eyes, we are in the presence of God, who is love. We are at a listening point. As Blanche says in the arms of her lover in Tennessee Williams's *A Streetcar Named Desire*,

"Sometimes there is God—so quickly."

Yes, a listening point is frustratingly quick, but it is also God. God is the only permanence, and Jesus, the incarnation of God, is the proof. The way you keep your moments, the way you keep listening, is to find yourself loving. Heraclitus was wrong. The only constant is love. The command at the listening point is to love.

What is the first thing Jesus does when he comes down from the mountain? So often we read the Bible out of context. We take a passage and isolate it in a booth when what went before and what comes after should be in the booth as well. What went before was that Jesus loved so much that he told his disciples he would have to go to Jerusalem and be killed. And what comes after was that Jesus loved so much that he healed a boy with epilepsy.

If the only constant is love, as Jesus taught, then the way you make your booth, the way you keep your loving moments, the way you keep your call, is to keep on loving. Jesus came down from what Abraham Maslow would have called a "peak experience" only to experience more peaks. It is a mountaintop experience, a new high, whenever we love. God arrives when we love. "A new commandment I give to you," Jesus says to Peter and the other disciples, "that you love one another" (Jn 13:34).

The way you keep the car from forever vanishing down the driveway is to keep on loving. The way you keep your child's vacant bedroom from remaining forever vacant is to keep on loving. The way you keep your departed loved one alive is to keep on loving. Peter knew that the only constant is love after the resurrection, the most loving act in history. We too are on the other side of the resurrection, so we know the only constant is love.

I was calling once in the home of a parishioner. An elderly loved one had died, and the family was sharing moments from this loved one's life. As I drove away I said to myself, *This is all there is. Deep moments like these are what life is all about.* We had lost track of time. You know it's a loving moment if you lose track of time. The room in which we were sitting seemed to have taken on a glow. My friends' faces seemed ever so slightly transfigured. We were transfixed. A moment of time stood still.

But it was the going away that brought the revelation. So often our theology is in retrospect. I drove away with the radio off and felt God had revealed that the way the people in the home and I were going to keep the moment was to keep on loving as many people as possible in future moments. That way there would be an enduring moment. That way life would not pass like a shadow but be illuminated by love.

You Realize There Is No Love Without Pain
But what happens when your frustration is greatest, when the loved one goes down the driveway for the last time, when the last corner is turned, the last handkerchief waved, the door on the bedroom closed? Then you will keep all the moments of love with your loved one by finding yourself loving others. To love is to love is to love.

Peter did not understand that love was the truth about life until he had gone to Jerusalem with Jesus and watched him be taken away and had experienced the resurrection. It seems as though we all have to go to Jerusalem. Peter did not understand that the only constant is love until Jesus, his loved one, had suffered—and until he, Peter, had suffered in losing and then denying his loved one.

If there are no tears, there is no love. If it doesn't hurt, it isn't love. It seems as though the way of glory is the way of the cross. The so-called theology of glory is reached through the theology of the cross. Perhaps that is why the Gospel writers put Jesus' great statement about following him just before the transfiguration and just after his announcement that he has to go to Jerusalem and "suffer many things" (Mk 8:31). "If any want to become my followers, let them deny themselves and take up their cross and follow me" (8:34 NRSV).

The glory of the transfiguration occurs in the Bible only after Jesus speaks of the agony of the cross, for himself and for others. The way of love that loves so much it will suffer if need be for the loved one—that is the way, the truth and the life. It is only as we suffer for our love that the way of love as the truth about life is revealed. That is why the tears in the driveway are the necessary work of love. "Was it not necessary," Jesus asks, "that the Christ should suffer these things and enter into his glory?" (Lk 24:26) "And he began to teach them that the Son of man must suffer many things" (Mk 8:31).

That there is no love without pain is the frustrating truth we learn as

we come down from the heights to obey our call to love in the depths.
Jesus knew that he and his three disciples could not stay on the heights.
They had to come down off the mountain and get their feet dirty. The
incarnation of love occurred in a stable. Our demonstrations of love occur
not only as we climb the heights of love with our loved ones, but as we
enter the depths of love with them and our epileptic boys.

Yes, there is a way to keep the lasting in the fleeting. God is the only
permanence. And God, the Bible says, is love. So if you want to keep your
loved ones forever, just keep on loving. If you want to hold the precious
moments of life, like those in which you hear a call, just keep on loving.

21

CALLS COME IN
PREJUDICE

The Woman at the Well

Y*ou have no doubt tried at one time or another to convert someone to* your way of thinking. A woman at a well in Samaria tried to convert Jesus. Little did she know that their discussion would bring her to a listening point, where she would hear the call of God and plumb the depths of her soul.

You Are Asked to Do Something for Christ
It is noon. Jesus is sitting by a well to rest while his disciples have gone into town to buy food. A woman comes to draw water, and Jesus asks her for a drink.

If you are to arrive at a listening point, the story suggests, it is because Jesus is asking you to do something for him. To whom can you give a cup of cold water? Whose life is parched? Who needs the living water that only Christ can give?

The woman declines to help. She is that full of prejudice. "How is it," she asks, "that you, a Jew, ask a drink of me, a woman of Samaria?" (Jn 4:9) She was a Samaritan, and Jews and Samaritans hated each other. As John explains to his Greek readers, "Jews have no dealings with Samaritans," primarily because Samaritans were open to marrying outside the faith.

The story of the woman at the well suggests that if there were any one thing Jesus needs us to do for him it is to combat prejudice of every stripe. The world is thirsty for openness, tolerance and unbiased, unprejudiced living with one another—from South Africa to the South Bronx.

The disciples were aghast that Jesus was talking to the woman at the well. "They marveled that he was talking with a woman" (Jn 4:27). Such a thing just wasn't done. Rabbis were forbidden to speak to women in public, even to their own wives or sisters. If they did, it was the end of their reputation. Jesus was not a rabbi, of course, but he was viewed by many as such. So here we have another cultural absolutism guaranteeing prejudice.

Instead, You Argue About Religion

Jesus asks us to meet his need. We decline to help because we are prejudiced against him. But he will not leave it at that. He knows our prejudice can be a potential listening point.

If the woman at the well wants to ignore his need, he will go along. He knows that her arguing with him is important if she is ever going to hear his need as her call. She asks him three questions and comes up with six arguments: One, you're a Jew and I'm a Samaritan. Two, you're a man and I'm a woman; we shouldn't even be talking. Three, are you better than Jacob, who gave us this well of seeping water while you are proposing running water? Four, "I have no husband," which was true but deceptive, since she had had five (Jn 4:18). Five, this is the place to worship, at the bottom of this mountain, not in Jerusalem—another absolutism. Six, a Messiah is coming who will support my arguments.

Ask your questions. Advance your arguments. Be honest about who you are. The only way Jesus wants us is "just as we are, without one plea." Don't be so impatient to hear a call that you shortchange the process and miss a possible listening point.

In his novel *Zorba the Greek*, Nikos Kazantzakis tells of just such a shortchange:

I discovered a cocoon in the bark of a tree. I waited a while, but it was too long appearing and I was impatient. I bent over it and breathed on it to warm it. . . . The miracle began to happen before my eyes, faster than life. The case opened, the butterfly started slowly crawling out, and I shall never forget my horror when I saw how its wings were folded back and crumpled. . . .

Bending over it, I tried to help it with my breath. In vain. It needed to be hatched out patiently, and the unfolding of the wings should be a gradual process in the sun. Now it was too late. My breath had forced the butterfly to appear, all crumpled, before its time. It struggled desperately and, a few second later, died in the palm of my hand.

Be Prepared for Counterarguments

When you argue with Jesus about answering his call for help, you must be ready for him to argue back. Progressively he deepens the argument. The woman doesn't realize what he is doing.

Jesus tells her he can give her "living water" (Jn 4:10). He means eternal life, but she is not ready to hear that yet. "Sir, you have nothing to draw with, and the well is deep; where do you get that living water?" (4:11)

Her objection doesn't bother him. She is there, and he is there, and they have all the time they need. He also has all the time he needs for us. All that matters is that the events of life, like this chance encounter at a well, gradually bring us to a listening point, where we can hear Jesus after arguing with him and telling him we are not the one to meet his need or answer his call.

"Sir," she says, "give me this water, that I may not thirst, nor come here to draw" (4:15). She thinks of the living water as a stream running by her house day and night. All she would have to do would be to reach out her hand and dip.

"Go," Jesus says, "call your husband" (4:16). She says that she has no husband, which is true, but what she does not say is that she is living with a man and has had five husbands before this man. Her sin is her idolatry of pleasure or change or self-gratification or all three.

Jesus brings her sin to light. Whenever you have Jesus even remotely in your life, you run the risk of his revealing the sinful side of yourself that you don't like and are defensive about with your questions and arguments.

The story is telling us that it is precisely when we are most defensive that we may be at a listening point.

But the woman at the well parries, defensive to the end: "Sir, I perceive you are a prophet" (4:19). Then she is off again on another absolutist argument about the best place to worship God, hoping that it will deflect him from making her deal with her sin. But his exposing of her sin and thus his revealing of her inner self is beginning to work.

You Cannot Hide Forever

We can only hide so long. Prejudice, defensiveness and argument are nothing more than dodges to keep us from dealing with our inmost selves. But confrontation with Christ in prayer or Bible reading or with someone who is Christlike won't let us get away with dodging. Indeed, it is the very dodging itself that is bringing us to a listening point. That is why, whenever we find ourselves being prejudiced, defensive or argumentative, it could be a listening point.

"I know that Messiah is coming," the woman says. "I who speak to you am he," Jesus replies (Jn 4:25-26). With that, she is at her listening point.

She runs back to town so fast she forgets her water jar. "Come," she cries to her friends, "see a man who told me all that I ever did" (4:29). He has revealed her to herself. He has given her her inmost self. He has put her in touch with her soul. Now she is whole, at peace, at least for the moment.

Her only instinct is to tell people about the revealer. At last she is giving him the help he wants. Our call is to tell others how Jesus has revealed us to ourselves.

Her friends and neighbors come out of the city in droves. They invite him to town. He stays two days. "Many Samaritans from that city believed in him because of the woman's testimony" (4:39). It was astonishing.

She never did give him a drink.

22

CALLS COME IN ARROGANCE

Job

T he book of Job is commonly read as the story of a good man who had bad things happen to him but who remained close to God to the end. He lost his health, his wealth and his children, but he never lost his God. So goes the conventional wisdom.

You Argue with God

The fact is, Job takes God on at every turn, castigating God for allowing such terrible things to happen to him, indeed for having caused them to happen. "Behold, he will slay me," Job says in a frequently mistranslated verse. "I have no hope; yet I will defend my ways to his face" (Job 13:15). The King James Version erroneously translates, "Though he slay me, yet will I trust in him." But Job's message is much angrier:

I will not restrain my mouth . . .
  I will complain in the bitterness of my soul. . . .
Thou dost scare me with dreams
  and terrify me with visions, . . .
  Why hast thou made me thy mark?
  Why have I become a burden to thee? (7:11, 14, 20)

So it goes for the rest of the book.

The one thing Job valued more than anything, more even than God, was his vaunted "integrity." "Till I die," he cries, "I will not put away my integrity from me. I hold fast my righteousness, and will not let it go; my heart does not reproach me for any of my days" (Job 27:5-6).

Job is arrogant. That is his problem. That is why he cannot hear God. The reason God deals him blow after blow is to humble him, to humiliate him to the point where he can at last reach a listening point. Ironically, Job thought he had been hearing God call all along. "I had heard of thee by the hearing of the ear," he says. But he realizes his hearing was only hearsay. "Now my eye sees thee; therefore I despise myself, and repent in dust and ashes" (42:5-6).

It takes the entire book to bring Job to his listening point. It takes all the vicissitudes of his life. The trouble with his three friends, all of whom bring him both good and bad theological advice, is that they arrive too early. Job cannot hear God yet. He is not ready for their theology. Apparently he has not experienced enough, not even with the loss of his health, wealth and children.

The trouble with the positive experiences of life is that they can feed our natural tendency to be arrogant. They have happened to us, we may feel, because we are capable. We deserve them. Job had had plenty of such experiences. The trouble with negative experiences is that they can feed our equally natural tendency to despair. We may feel they have happened to us unjustly. We are without hope and hence without God.

All had been well with Job. "There is none like him on the earth," God says to Satan, "a blameless and upright man, who fears God and turns away from evil" (2:3). You can't have a more positive life than that. Such a life was like that of Adam and Eve. The only trouble was that his comfortable lifestyle with a wife and four children had not brought him to a listening point. That was why God had to use Satan, the avatar of the negative, to get Job to a place where he could, for the first time, hear God's call.

Your Suffering Makes You Receptive to God
Suffering can position us for a call. It can get us to a listening point.

"When a man believes himself to be utterly lost," Luther said, "light breaks."[1] Manna came to the Israelites *in the wilderness*. Angels came to Jesus *in his temptations*. Ravens came to Elijah *in his exile*. God gets through to Job *in his sufferings*.

It is our suffering that can purge us of our arrogance and self-righteousness and bring us to a listening point. Perhaps that is why God tells Ananias, in speaking about the arrogant Paul, "I will show him how much he must suffer for the sake of my name" (Acts 9:16). It may also be why Jesus said, "If any want to become my followers, let them deny themselves and take up their cross and follow me" (Mk 8:34 NRSV).

It is his suffering that eventually brings Job to one of the great listening points in the Bible. God speaks for four chapters, the longest speech of God in the Bible. It is withering in its sarcasm to one who had said, "like a prince I would approach him" (Job 31:37):

> Where were you when I laid the foundation of the earth?
> Tell me, if you have understanding.
> Who determined its measurements—surely you know! . . .
> Have you commanded the morning since your days began? . . .
> Have you entered into the springs of the sea? . . .
> Have the gates of death been revealed to you? . . .
> Declare, if you know all this. (Job 38:4-5, 12, 16-18)

With his arrogance purged by his suffering, Job is at last in position to hear God's call. He, the upper-middle-class executive who had his business, family and community life in impeccable order, had experienced everything in life except suffering, and so had not yet experienced God. He knew about God, but he had not yet known God.

With the suffering, what he had known by hearsay he now knew by experience. Religion is the direct experience of God. "Theology," wrote Coventry Patmore, "is the science of self-evident reality." God becomes evident through suffering. God is experienced through suffering.

The Suffering of Jesus Shows How Suffering Brings God

Jesus also knew the value of suffering in experiencing God. "The Son of man must suffer many things," he says to the disciples immediately after

Peter affirms him as the Christ (Mk 8:31). His Christness cannot be separated from his suffering, which is why Christians have seen the Suffering Servant as personified in Jesus. Jesus knew the value of suffering in experiencing God's call was a hard idea, so Mark adds that "he said this plainly" (8:32). But Peter cannot believe it and argues with Jesus, whereupon Jesus uses his harshest language: "Get behind me, Satan!" (8:33)

We can only infer that a sonship without suffering was the greatest threat to the mission of the Son. It was satanic for Peter to think that Jesus could be the Christ without suffering. Being a nonsuffering servant was a temptation to which Jesus dare not succumb. God can be talked about and thought about without suffering, but God can often be experienced only through whatever suffering is necessary to humble us to the point where we can, at last, hear God call.

Experiencing God through suffering was also the experience of the Hebrew people, which Job should have known and which Jesus was later to personify. They suffered in Egypt, in the wilderness, in the Promised Land. But their suffering was always for a purpose—to bring them to their listening points. It strains credulity that suffering can be purposeful, but that is the point the Bible is making. Its purpose is to give the sufferer a direct experience of God by purging the sufferer of his or her natural arrogance, at least for a while, at least for the duration of the suffering.

Suffering did what repeated calls could not do. The calls did not go through because the Israelites were not ready to hear. They were arrogant. "You have been rebellious against the LORD from the day that I knew you," God says (Deut 9:24). "From the day you came out of the land of Egypt, until you came to this place, you have been rebellious against the LORD" (9:7). The only way to defeat such "princely" arrogance is through suffering.

That is why the Bible will even go so far as to say that God causes suffering, as when God hands Job over to Satan for the express purpose of making him suffer. "Behold, he is in your power," God says (Job 2:6). "He humbled you and let you hunger . . . that he might make you know that man does not live by bread alone" (Deut 8:3).

God humbles an arrogant Job, using suffering as the agent of his humiliation. It works. Job is no longer arrogant. "I have uttered what I did not understand," he confesses. "Therefore I despise myself, and repent in dust and ashes" (Job 42:3, 6). At last he is at a listening point.

You can be too, because of whatever you may be suffering.

Part V

CALLS ARE HEARD IN EVERYDAY EXPERIENCES

23

CALLS COME IN HABIT

Daniel

O ne of the best ways to arrive at a listening point is to find yourself practicing your religion regularly. If you are in the habit of listening for God, you may hear God when you need him most.

The Habit of Prayer

Daniel was at the zenith of his career, but that did not deter him from practicing his religion regularly. "Daniel became distinguished above all the other presidents," the Bible says. Indeed, "the king planned to set him over the whole kingdom" (Dan 6:3). It was quite an achievement for one so young—and a captured foreigner at that.

However, as we will see in the case of Saul, the higher one rises the more jealousies one provokes. The other officials plot Daniel's overthrow. They concoct a scheme to ask the king to promulgate a thirty-day law forbidding the petitioning of any god or man but the king. Anyone not obeying the law would be thrown into the lions' den.

Daniel's response to the crisis is exemplary. The Bible says he "got down upon his knees three times a day and prayed and gave thanks before his God, as he had done previously" (6:10). The whole call is in the five words, "as he had done previously." Daniel makes the pages of history because he finds himself on his knees three times a day in good times and bad. The crisis comes and it becomes a listening point.

The king now regrets his law but has to go through with the punishment. He says to Daniel, "May your God, whom you serve continually, deliver you!" (6:16) Again, Daniel's whole religion is in those four words, "whom you serve continually." The king was aware of Daniel's steadfastness. In the same way, your God whom you are in the habit of serving, your God to whom you pray each day, your God whom you remember with every morsel you eat, that God will save you in your moment of peril.

Your Habits Are Learned in Your Family of Origin

What do you find yourself doing continually that might bring you to a listening point? Whatever it is, the story of Daniel suggests, it has to be continual or it will not position you to hear the call of God in your next crisis. It has to be habitual or it will not be strong enough to bind you to God in bad times as well as good. Religious habit is not the only way to arrive at a listening point, of course, but it is certainly one, and a good one.

Daniel was ready for the bad because he had prepared in the good. When he was at the zenith he was preparing for the nadir. When life is good and I am at the peak of my career, that is when my religious habits are preparing me for the automobile accident, the office intrigue, the death in the family, my own terminal illness.

Brother Lawrence wrote a remarkable little book in the seventeenth century called *The Practice of the Presence of God*. It is still being sold. One reason for its popularity is the word *practice*. Brother Lawrence reached the point where he could hear God calling in the most mundane tasks of life, such as washing the dishes. One reason he could hear was that he practiced listening.

We have said that it takes nothing more than the events of life to bring us to a listening point. In Daniel's case, we infer his being brought up in a religious family because of his religious habits as a young man. He found himself keeping the dietary laws and the habit of prayer he had learned at home and thus staying in touch with God. His religious habits were so much a part of him that he kept them even after being kidnapped and thrown into an alien culture that practiced an entirely different religion.

The word for *habit* in religion is *ritual.* Finding himself in daily touch with God had become a ritual for Daniel. That is why it was a good bet that he would be able to hear the call of God in a crisis. Indeed, on his return from the lions' den, he explains to the king why his life was spared. "My God sent his angel and shut the lions' mouths," he reports (Dan 6:22).

The word *ritual* comes from the root for "fit together." The purpose of religious ritual is to fit things together in life—events, people, good and bad times. With what Brother Lawrence called practicing the presence of God, things begin to fit. *Ritual* also has the same root as *arithmetic.* With ritual we can begin to see how things are adding up and how we are being moved toward a potential listening point.

Your Life Can Unravel Without the Habit of Prayer

Robert Bellah's celebrated book *Habits of the Heart* bears a title taken from Alexis de Tocqueville, who, on his tour of America in the 1840s, discovered what he called certain "habits of the heart"—in religion, economics and politics—that made Americans what they were. The key to understanding Americans, he wrote, was not our ideas so much as our habits. These three habits were intertwined, but now, Bellah suggests, they are becoming unraveled. Public life is separated from private. Individuals are separated from community. The workplace is separated from the family. And many of us are separated from religion.

One reason for the unraveling of American life is that we have lost many of our rituals. We have lost the sense that religion, economics and politics fit together. One reason we have lost such a sense is that our families no longer practice their religion as habitually as Daniel's family did.

One ritual families do practice religiously, of course, is watching television. According to the A. C. Nielsen ratings company, the average child aged two to eleven watches a mind-boggling 3.91 hours a day. By the time most young people leave high school, they have spent more time in front of their TV than in front of their teachers.

From where does the motivation come for keeping the religious rituals, such as praying and reading the Bible and going to worship? As with

Daniel, the answer is from God through your family of origin; if not from your family, then from any number of things that may happen to you: being far from home, in a crisis, at the zenith of your career.

And what if there were no such motivation? You could still arrive at a listening point. You cannot limit God. You cannot limit the action of the Holy Spirit: "The wind blows where it wills" (Jn 3:8). The story of Daniel suggests simply this: that hearing the call of God, particularly in a crisis, may well be easier if you find yourself getting down on your knees three times a day and praying and giving thanks before your God, as you have done previously.

24

CALLS COME IN WORSHIP

Isaiah

Isaiah *was well educated, moved in the best circles, belonged to the ruling* class. Active in politics, with a particular interest in foreign policy, he was married, had children, was steeped in his religion and worshiped regularly. He also left a dramatic account of how, in the year 742 B.C., he came to a listening point and heard God call.

Worship Kindles the Imagination
The call came in a worship service. As Isaiah described it: "In the year that King Uzziah died I saw the Lord sitting upon a throne, high and lifted up; and his train filled the temple. . . . And the foundations of the thresholds shook at the voice of him who called" (Is 6:1-4).

The worship service kindled his imagination. "Imagination is more important than knowledge," Einstein said. "When the pioneers in science send forth the groping feelers of their thoughts," Max Planck wrote, "they must have vivid intuitive imaginations, for new ideas are not generated by deduction, but by an artistically creative imagination."

"I just walk a great deal over the countryside," says America's most famous artist, Andrew Wyeth. "I try to leave myself very blank."

When did you last come to a worship service blank?

"The purpose of a play," said Tyrone Guthrie, "is to try to interest the members of an audience so intensely that they are rapt, taken 'out' of themselves"—as Isaiah was. Wyeth is so rapt in his walks that he loses himself. "Damp rotting leaves and moisture," he writes of Halloween, "smell of make-up. As a child, the smell inside a pumpkin when a candle is lit. The feel of your face under a mask walking down a road in the moonlight. I love all that, because then I don't exist anymore."

And when I don't exist, God can. Those who lose their lives for his sake, Jesus said, will find them (Mt 10:39). When you find yourself lost in worship you can be found by God. Isn't that what hearing the Word and closing your eyes and raising your voice and listening to the music is supposed to do?

Worship Stimulates Self-Awareness

Isaiah finds himself moved from his stunning awareness of God to an equally stunning awareness of himself. "Woe is me! For I am lost; for I am a man of unclean lips, and I dwell in the midst of a people of unclean lips; for my eyes have seen the King, the LORD of hosts!" (Is 6:5)

His awareness of God immediately brings him awareness of himself in his worst as well as his best, but the worst comes first. Without God there is no sense of sin. "Man is the measure of all things," Protagoras boasted. But the psalmist asks God, "What is man that thou art mindful of him?" (Ps 8:4)

Say you are well educated, move in the best circles, belong to the ruling class. Say you are active in politics, are married and have children, are steeped in your religion and worship regularly. Life is good. It could always be better, of course, but things are going well. You are comfortable and happy. Could it be that your sin is that you know no sin? That you have no imagination for the worst as well as the best of who you are? That your awareness of God is insufficient to stoke your imagination about yourself?

"The beauty of building the church inside the prison," writes former Watergate figure Charles Colson, "is that in the prison they don't fall for the three things I think are the cultural traps into which the church has fallen." The first, he says, is viewing the church "as a building, a place, a structure, bricks, mortar." The second is that "the church more and more is seen as a place for therapy, to make you feel good. When did Jesus ever tell people he would make them feel good?" The third is that the church errs by linking success with bigness. "Pastors," he says, "are under terrible pressure from the laity to grow at all costs," to the point that their members want them to preach "a good message" to attract crowds rather than emphasize the need to repent.

Worship Brings Forgiveness

A third step in Isaiah's hearing the call of God follows hard on awareness and confession. No sooner does Isaiah realize he is lost than he discovers he is found. God acts most imaginatively.

"Then flew one of the seraphim to me, having in his hand a burning coal which he had taken with tongs from the altar. And he touched my mouth, and said: 'Behold, this has touched your lips; your guilt is taken away, and your sin is forgiven' " (Is 6:6-7).

Confession was never an isolated act for the Hebrews. It was always preceded by adoration and succeeded by thanksgiving. They praised God for deliverance from Egypt. Then they confessed their unworthiness to have been delivered because of their subsequent rebellion. Then they thanked God for removing their guilt and forgiving their sin.

The burning coal on Isaiah's lips was a symbol of God's gracious act of forgiveness. But it comes only after his confession, and his confession comes only after the objective jolt of his call. The imaginative act of confessing his separation from God put him in position to have the separation overcome by God in forgiveness. In other words, there can be no forgiveness if there is no sin, and there can be no sin if there is no God, and there can be no awareness of God if there is no imagination. The call comes to the imagination.

Worship Brings Your Orders

A final step in hearing the call is Isaiah's commission. It is in his commission that the power of the call is perhaps most evident. "And I heard the voice of the Lord saying, 'Whom shall I send, and who will go for us?' Then I said, 'Here am I! Send me!' And he said, 'Go' " (Is 6:8-9).

The power of forgiveness is such that anyone who experiences it wants to do something for the forgiver. Isaiah was a forgiven man. That is why he could stand out alone against his people and call them to repentance. He had the strength that goes with forgiveness. The disciples were forgiven. Paul was forgiven. That is why they were lost in their calls and were able to go about them so imaginatively.

The converted Isaiah has his commission, to preach the good news of repentance before it is too late. We have the same commission, to share the good news about hearing God call, but we are going to need our imaginations stoked to obey it.

Anything goes to stoke our imaginations when it comes to God. Confession, forgiveness and commissioning are not going to occur without that initial, powerful awareness of God. Such awareness could come anywhere, anytime. For Isaiah it came in a worship service. But he had been in that same worship service in that same temple hundreds of times. Why did the call come this time?

It came because the circumstances of his life had at last enabled him to hear. They had brought him to a listening point. What were these circumstances? We will never know for sure because Isaiah does not say, but we have a good idea. The foreign policy of his country, which he had a hand in defining, was going awry. Indeed, in only twenty years his country would be obliterated and would not appear again until 1948.

It had been a personal and national crisis that brought him to his listening point. The word *crisis* comes from the root for "turning point." His listening point became a turning point as he heard God ask, "Whom shall I send, and who will go for us?" He would go because he couldn't not go. "Necessity is laid upon me," Paul writes. "Woe to me if I do not preach the gospel!" (1 Cor 9:16)

Abraham had to go to the Promised Land. Moses had to go back to Egypt. Paul had to preach. Once you are called you are under orders to do something for God. It is your divine vocation. Remember, to hear in Hebrew means to obey. You have been given something you must do. You can't not do it and still be yourself.

Many in late-twentieth-century America are looking everywhere for the "authentic self," but what people fail to realize is that it is right here, at the point of their call. Many are looking for their "true vocation in life," but what they fail to realize is that their vocation is waiting for them at the next worship service.

All it takes is for the imagination to be detonated. Anything can set it off. But we have to be ready. That is to say, we have to be readied by the events of life that bring us to our particular crises. Fortunately, the events of life are in the process of doing just that all the time.

25

CALLS COME IN CONTEMPLATING SCRIPTURE

A Psalmist

Jesus *remained true to his call by invoking the Word of God.* Ezekiel remained true to his by eating God's scroll in his vision (Ezek 3:3). Ezra urged the Israelites to be true to theirs by reading them the book of the law of Moses (Neh 8:1-10).

From the law of Moses came the Shema Israel, "Hear, O Israel," second only to the Ten Commandments in importance, to be taught, repeated, pondered and worn on the hand and between the eyes as a reminder to the Hebrew people of their call to be God's servants (Deut 6:4-9).

Hence a psalmist writes, "Great are the works of the LORD; they are pondered by all who delight in them" (Ps 111:2 NIV). Likewise, Luke records that "Mary kept all these things, pondering them in her heart" (Lk 2:19).

Pondering the Bible is the centuries-old *lectio divina*, or divine reading. It is something we can do every day. We can find ourselves contemplating a thought, image or feeling in the Bible that catches our attention. We can ponder it. And we can hear ourselves called when we do. As St. Augustine said, "O Lord, Thou didst strike my heart with Thy Word, and I loved Thee."

What Is Pondering?

What does it mean to find yourself pondering? To ponder means to seek out the inner meaning, investigate, question, research, study, read over, ruminate. As a cow chews its cud, so we chew on a particular passage in the Bible that has caught our attention. We roll it around as a good wine. Ezekiel was told to "eat" the divine words in the form of the scroll.

To contemplate means "to consider the signs in [a] sacred area," such as a temple.[1] In this definition a temple was an open space marked out for observation by ancient priests called augurs, a place reserved, sacred, holy, "cut out" from all other space, stretching from earth to sky.[2] The augur would observe what was going on in this sacred space in order to divine the intentions of the gods and so be able to issue an augury, an announcement about the future.

Thus, to contemplate means to take a long, hard look at something (the prefix *con* meaning "intense" or "long"),[3] particularly something that has come to our attention in a sacred space, such as the Bible, or any space in which we find ourselves looking for what God has in mind for us. The Bible is a sacred space, or temple, cut out from all other spaces for our observation, our contemplation, our pondering.

Why Ponder the Bible?

Why do we ponder the Bible? What is the motivation for entering into its sacred space? "The word of God is living and active," the writer of Hebrews affirms, "sharper than any two-edged sword, piercing to the division of soul and spirit, of joints and marrow, and discerning the thoughts and intentions of the heart. And before him no creature is hidden, but all are open and laid bare to the eyes of him with whom we have to do" (Heb 4:12-13).

The Bible lays us bare. It discerns the thoughts and intentions of the heart. It gets us down to the inner core of who we are, where the truth about ourselves resides, where we stand alone before God, the one "to whom we must render an account" (4:13 NRSV).

The Bible reminds us that we are not to fritter our lives away in pursuing false gods, false calls, false senses of self. It reminds us rather to contemplate the works of the Lord. Without the Bible, we might never study them. Without the Bible, we might never move into sacred space because all space would be secular, one-dimensional, human only.

The Bible has its own drawing power. We are moved to pick it up because we know that it knows us. We know that the truth about ourselves is there. We know that it is in the Bible—among other places, of course—that we can meet God, that the thoughts and intentions of God's heart can become known to us, as good augurs, if we will but ponder.

How Do You Ponder the Bible?

There are as many ways to ponder the Bible as there are people, but few ways have stood the test of time as well as the *lectio divina*. The divine reading suggests, first, that you cut out your holy space, physically and temporally. Physically, it should be some place in the home or workplace that is right. A chair with a table, a chair alone, your bed, your desk, wherever. But it should be a place that you connect with this particular activity, so you can contemplate with the fewest distractions and the most good feeling.

Temporally, it should be a time that is right—a time when you are relaxed, ready, open. That may not be first thing in the morning when you are racing to start your day. Then again, it may be. It may not be the last thing at night when you are so relaxed that you find yourself missing what you are reading. However, the wisdom of the ages tends to suggest that these are, indeed, two good times, so they are at least worth considering.

The physical and temporal have to be right because you are preparing to meet your God in your God's sacred space and in the temple of your own room or work space, which makes it one of the most important times of your day. Reading the Bible is not like reading a book or the newspaper. With the premise that it is God's Word and that we are being laid bare when we read it, the stakes are high. We approach the Bible with what is called a "high view of Scripture."

With this in mind, I would suggest one thing to add to your physical arrangement—a red pencil. This way your Bible becomes yours. You underline everything that speaks to you; if it speaks with particular power, you might want to copy it into the front of the book.

Or if you prefer because of your high view of Scripture, you might want to have two Bibles, one that you read with great reverence at your reading place and another that you mark up.

Go Slow

Second, go slow. If you have read more than a few verses and have not underlined anything, then you are probably going too fast. Reading too fast is perhaps the biggest single mistake we make with the Bible. Reading fast is, by definition, inimical to pondering. You cannot begin to observe everything going on in the sacred space of the Bible and the sacred space of your own self in relation to the Bible if you read faster than a few words or phrases or sentences a minute. When I was in a small group that met weekly to read the Gospel of John, we discovered that it took us an average of five weeks to read one chapter.

"Be still, and know that I am God" (Ps 46:10). Go slow, and know. Dawdle. Go down the side roads. Contemplate the landscape. Take in everything. Stroll through the Bible. Saunter. Imagine you are walking with a three-year-old, where everything is fresh and new.

Stop Often

Reading the Bible this way, you will find yourself constantly stopping, arrested by things seen for the first time. Use your red pencil to stop your headlong rush to finish the paragraph or chapter. Stop when the first word or phrase or image or feeling arrests you. A pondering psalm begins with the simple sentence, "Praise the Lord." You might find yourself stopping right there, struck, as Mary was, by all the things you have in your life for which to praise the Lord. "Mary kept all these things, pondering them in her heart" (Lk 2:19).

I was taking care of some children one morning in a church I served, and we were walking around getting acquainted with the sacred space and with each other. We stopped by the baptism bowl to look at the dove. We stopped in the sacristy to look at the water from the Jordan River and the pebbles from the Sea of Galilee. We stopped in front of the communion table to try to decipher the carvings of the twelve apostles. We stopped to stand in the pulpit and read the inscription, "We would see Jesus."

Stop your reading. Close your eyes. Contemplate what you have just read. Ponder it. See how it is bringing you into sacred space. Hear what it is trying to say to you. Do what it is telling you to do. Then do the same on Sundays. During the reading of the sacred words in the sacred space, why not close your eyes and contemplate what is being read? Stop at the first word or phrase or image or feeling that arrests you. Ponder it.

Take the Word with You

Carry the word, phrase, thought, image or feeling that has caught your attention into your day. Lay it as a template on everything you do. A template is a metal cutout used as a guide in replication, like a cookie cutter.

The psalmist is asking us to ponder the works of the Lord as an overlay on everything we do. See your child as a work of the Lord, as well as your spouse, your job, your fellow employees, your food. I once heard a rabbi tell a group of Christians that Jews try to see everything during the day as a work of the Lord, right down to the bare details.

In Psalm 111 the writer reminds the Jews of particular works—food on the flight from Egypt, commandments on Mt. Sinai, the nation itself cut out as sacred space in the heart of the Middle East, redemption as they are returned from Babylon after years of exile: "Great are the works of the Lord; they are pondered by all who delight in them" (Ps 111:2 NIV). It echoes like a refrain throughout your day as you ponder the incredible things that have happened to you in your life—your rescue from whatever bondage you have experienced, your return after a time of exile from God, from others, from your inner self.

The Word of God works as a template on our nights too. As we read it before going to sleep, it mingles with the unconscious and works its way into our dreams, converting the riot of images from the day into a new sacred space, a new temple, in which new "augurs" are at work divining the thoughts and intentions of the heart.

But the Word of God will work as a template only when we have been moved to pick it up in the first place because of a feeling that we may be frittering our lives away by living in one-dimensional, secular, human space only. When that feeling comes, it should be no surprise to find yourself pulling a rarely opened book off a shelf, proceeding slowly, stopping frequently, contemplating, chewing, rolling the taste of the words around in your mouth, as you observe, fascinated, all that is going on in the sacred space.

26

CALLS COME IN
INTERRUPTION
The Good Samaritan

Everyone remembers the story of the Good Samaritan, but few remember that Jesus told it in response to a man's question, "What shall I do to inherit eternal life?" (Lk 10:25) Jesus answers, in effect, "Act like the Good Samaritan."

His answer is perplexing because we learned long ago that Christians are justified by faith, not by works, but here Jesus is saying that the way we get eternal life is by the way we act. How then did the Good Samaritan act?

You Do Not Have to Go Out of Your Way to Be Called

The Good Samaritan did not set about to do good, he simply went about his life. He was doing what he always did, namely, make occasional business trips to Jerusalem. We infer such trips because his credit was good at the inn. He was known, and he would be back.

The Good Samaritan did not go out of his way to help someone in need; the person in need was in his way. He chanced upon him as part of his daily routine. Your neighbor, Jesus is saying, is someone you don't have to go out of your way to find. He or she will suddenly be there as you go about your life. Your call will come as you go about your life.

I have a friend who simply could not get along with a coworker. Nor could anyone else. After trying everything, my friend felt called, as she told it to me, to "love her to death." Within a few weeks the employees were calling the office "Camelot."

You Do Not Have to Know or Like the One You Help

The Good Samaritan found himself helping someone he would not normally help. Jews and Samaritans hated each other. Their hatred stemmed from the Samaritans' marrying outside their tribe and worshiping God on Mt. Gerizim. The Jews thought it better not to marry outside their tribe and to worship God on Mt. Zion.

There are just eight nations that existed in 1914 that have not had their form of government changed—the United Kingdom, four present or former members of the British Commonwealth, the United States, Sweden and Switzerland. Of the remaining 170 contemporary states, the most frequent factor in violent change has been ethnic conflict, often fueled by religion.

What we need around the world is a good dose of Good Samaritanism. What would that look like? You may be at odds with your employer, employee or customer over a minor matter blown completely out of proportion, or it could be a major matter blown sky-high because of inflammatory rhetoric. There may be something about a classmate, teacher or friend you cannot stand. You may be in a serious falling out with a spouse or family member. If you find yourself helping that other person, who at the moment is not your friend but is in your way, then, Jesus is saying, you will not only be answering a call, you will be on your way to eternal life.

Your Interruption Can Be Seen as Grace, Not Chance

The Good Samaritan found himself viewing his interruption as grace. Jesus presents this view in stark contrast to that of two others: a priest (someone presumably open to grace) and a Levite (an assistant priest). It was a chance for all three, but only one of them saw chance as grace.

When you start thinking about chance, you may be amazed by how it could be plan. I know a couple who met while polishing the piano at a workday at their church. They would be the first to say their subsequent marriage was due to grace, not chance. They might even go so far as to say chance was plan.

People drop into our lives all the time as we go about our daily routines, and the question they prompt is, Are we going to view them as arriving by chance or by grace? "We must allow ourselves to be interrupted by God," Dietrich Bonhoeffer said. But the priest and Levite viewed the man by the side of the road as an interruption only, not as an interruption from God, not as a signal that it was God calling them to act, which was Jesus' point.

Whenever an interruption breaks into your routine and you are suddenly confronted by someone you are hostile to, God could be calling. Doing something for that person, Jesus is saying, is how you will inherit eternal life, not just resting on your laurels as a believer in Christ. Believing without doing was one of the oldest heresies in the Christian church.

You Find Yourself Responding Spontaneously

The Good Samaritan found himself responding spontaneously. "When he saw him, he had compassion, and went to him" (Lk 10:33-34). There is something in the immediate, spontaneous response to someone in need that shouts *call* and hints *eternal life*.

Trust yourself. Trust your instincts. Instinctively we know that the way of love is the right way. The trouble is that we overlay our instincts with rationalizations for not doing what our instincts are telling us to do. It is the age-old conflict between Paul's "inmost self" and the outer self. The outer self dwells on the interruption and dislike, the inner self on the compassion. The outer self is prudential, counting the cost; the inner self is spontaneous, not counting the cost. The outer self calculates, the inner self acts. The outer self counters the call because it is God and not the self. It is something God is doing *through* the self. The inner self finds itself responding to the call because it sees God in the dying man at the side of the road.

A friend of mine has a daughter who has not spoken to him since his divorce from her mother; she didn't even invite him to her college graduation. How long is that going to go on? Is she going to let him pull her strings the rest of her life? He is in her way. He is part of her daily routine. She can't avoid him. How long will she play the priest and the Levite? How long will she resist God? When will she be able to respond spontaneously to her father? Only when time and events bring her to a listening point.

When you act spontaneously, you forget yourself in a moment of self-transcendence, as the Good Samaritan did. The priest, on the other hand, knew he would lose his job in the temple for seven days if he touched a dead person. Of course, he didn't know for sure that the man was dead, but it wasn't worth the risk. Nor was it for the Levite.

You Find Yourself Involved Totally

When you act spontaneously you also get involved totally. There is nothing halfway. The Good Samaritan binds the man's wounds, takes him to the inn and pays for his care. It costs him the equivalent of two days' wages, but he offers to pay even more on his return.

It is immediate, self-forgetful, total involvement. It is also living life, to the full. This is what life is all about. "I came that they may have life, and have it abundantly," Jesus said (Jn 10:10). The Good Samaritan is living abundantly.

All that you have is the present moment for living abundantly. As Billy Graham once said, "First, I lived for the day I would go to school. Then I lived for the day I would go to junior high. Then I lived for the day I would go to high school. Then I lived for the day I would go to college. Then I lived for the day I would get my first job. Then I lived for the day I would get married. Now I live just for today."

Love now. Love immediately, totally, self-forgetfully. As the song goes, "They'll know we are Christians by our love." And as Jesus said, "The tree is known by its fruit" (Mt 12:33). Jesus says the same thing at the end of Matthew, where he talks about separating the sheep from the goats and how those who inherit eternal life will be those who feed the hungry, clothe the naked, welcome the stranger, and visit the sick and imprisoned (25:31-46).

What is the difference between this position and the Pharisees' position that you can work your way to God by obeying the 613 laws of their religion? The difference is that it is not you who are doing the obeying. It is God working through you. There is no room for self-righteousness. We do not work our way to God; we work our way from God.

How do you know it is God? Because you wouldn't do it. There is no way you are going to answer the call, on your own, to love that offensive employee to death. You just aren't going to do it. If it is done, it has to be God; it can't be you because you wouldn't do it. And how do we know that? Because you haven't done it!

Grace is what happens to us. Grace is our response to what happens. Grace is what then happens through us. Grace is the wounded man by the side of the road. Grace is the Good Samaritan's finding himself responding. Grace is the binding of the man's wounds and taking him to the inn.

Jesus concludes the parable by saying, "Go and do likewise" (Lk 10:37). And you will—you will answer his call when you find yourself in immediate, total, self-forgetful involvement with an allegedly hostile person who has suddenly dropped into your everyday life.

27

CALLS COME IN
MENTORING

Paul

Stephen had been seized and taken before the high priest and the council. It is likely Paul was a member of this group. We are told that it was people from Cilicia, among others, who "arose and disputed with Stephen" (Acts 6:9), and, since Paul was from Cilicia and present only moments later at Stephen's death, it is safe to assume he was in the group arguing with Stephen.

You Resist Your Mentor

Are you resisting someone right now who could be the key to your call? Are you making talking points when you could be at a listening point? Is someone telling you, as Stephen told the council, that your God is too small?

Stephen showed the high priest and the council that they had limited God to their way of thinking about God. He tried to free them from such thinking, as your mentor is freeing you, only they did not want to be freed. It was like the Exodus from Egypt when the Israelites were "free at last," but all they could think about was going back, where at least they could count on a good meal.

Stephen cites chapter and verse for how the high priest and the council have limited God. Who has had the courage to do that for you? Who has dared to call you out of your parochialism? Stephen begins with the story of Abraham, reminding them how Abraham could not be limited to the piece of land known as Palestine, since he kept going in and out of it. The council, however, wanted to limit God to Israel's borders, and Stephen would have none of it. Abraham, he points out, had not even received his call within Israel's borders.

Stephen also turns to Israel's tendency to reject the very people sent to call them out of their limited way of viewing God. He tells the stories of Moses and Joseph and ends with the rejection of Jesus. Have you rejected the very person God may have sent to save you? Paul rejected Stephen, who had a very limited time to do his mentoring but still did it nonetheless.

Stephen shows Paul and the others how they have limited God not just to the land but to the temple. They had reduced the *shekinah*, the presence of God, to only one sacred space, the temple, and only one sacred space within the sacred space, the holy of holies, forgetting that the prophet had said, "Heaven is my throne, and earth my footstool" (Acts 7:49). Stephen's point is that God can be worshiped anywhere. You cannot limit God to your location of God. Paul had to hear that, but he could not grasp it yet, not until Stephen had finished his mentoring.

One often sees this limiting of God when people move away and say they cannot find another church like the one they have left. It's as though the presence of God had been limited to a particular space at a particular time in their lives. Who is your Stephen who will tell you, as Jesus did, that "something greater than the temple is here" (Mt 12:6)?

"You always resist the Holy Spirit," Stephen says to the council and high priest (Acts 7:51). You killed the prophets. You killed the one they prophesied. And you killed the law by failing to keep it. Every step of the way, from Abraham on, you have resisted the Holy Spirit. What was the Holy Spirit? It was everything that had been calling them out of their inveterate provincialism.

We too are provincial. We think of ourselves *and not others*. Thirty-five million Americans face life—and death—without health insurance. Five-

and-a-half-million children under the age of twelve don't have enough to eat. Only 2 percent of the $6.2 billion federal aid to education goes to school districts in which more than 75 percent of the students are poor. The Holy Spirit is what prevents our being provincial and limiting God to our specifications.

You Attack Your Mentor

Paul, the high priest and the council do not agree with Stephen. They cannot hear his call to enlarge their concept of God. They go on the attack. He has become a threat to purse and pride—purse because the temple was the economic center of the city, and pride because the law, even though they had not kept it, was what set them apart from everyone else on earth; it made their tribe unique.

"They were enraged," Luke reports, "and they ground their teeth against him" (Acts 7:54). But they were not yet a lynch mob. It remained for Stephen, "full of the Holy Spirit," to have a vision of Jesus in heaven "standing at the right hand of God," vindicating him, to turn them into a mob (7:55). "Then they cast him out of the city and stoned him; and the witnesses laid down their garments at the feet of a young man named Saul [Paul]" (7:58).

We attack the very person God has sent to be our mentor in the faith. We criticize. We judge. We exclude. We avoid. We will do anything to get him or her out of our lives. Why? Because he or she has shown us what we really are—greedy and haughty—and as such have limited God to our view of God.

Your Mentor Forgives You

But then a remarkable thing happens. Like Jesus, who said as he was being killed, "Father, forgive them; for they know not what they do" (Lk 23:34), Stephen prays, "Lord, do not hold this sin against them" (Acts 7:60). It staggers the imagination that anyone could do that while being killed. But that is what mentors do. They forgive the very ones who resist them and attack them. That is how they mentor. They are showing us how to lead the Christian life by the way they lead their own.

And no, their conduct does not necessarily make an impression the first time around. Your call may have to come around again and again, first at night perhaps, then at a business meeting, then over a meal at home. Stephen's conduct made so little impression on Paul at first that Paul goes even further on the attack by setting himself up as the premier hounder of Christians. "Saul was ravaging the church," the Bible records, "and entering house after house, he dragged off men and women and committed them to prison" (Acts 8:3).

It takes a while for forgiveness to work, perhaps because you cannot believe it is happening. When you have resisted all the way and then attacked the very person God has sent to call you from your parochialism, to be forgiven by that person is something beyond your ability to grasp, at least for a while.

It takes time for your mentor to be revealed. But time and events have a way of working. The very next mention of Paul is of his listening point on the road to Damascus (9:1-22). He has been moved from persecuting the church to joining it. The Holy Spirit, the very force he had resisted and attacked, has been at work.

Your Mentor Changes Your Life

Now Paul himself becomes a witness, as Stephen had been, and the calling process starts again. Paul will become a mentor in the faith. Stephen's death has given him new life. Indeed, it has given the whole church unexpected life. Stephen's death is the beginning of the worldwide mission of the church.

"The blood of the martyrs," goes an ancient saying, "is the seed of the church." Stephen, the first martyr, launches the first geometric expansion of the Christian church, in large part by launching Paul, the church's first great missionary. "The church owes Paul," St. Augustine said, "to the prayer of Stephen."

"Now those who were scattered went about preaching the word" (Acts 8:4). Wherever they were, they found themselves talking about Jesus. No one could stop them. *They* had become mentors, calling people out of their parochialism. They became so effective that a later mob was to say they had "turned the world upside down" (17:6).

Philip, one of these early Christians, while walking along the road finds himself drawn to a court official of the queen of Ethiopia who is reading Isaiah in his chariot. Philip asks him if he understands what he is reading, and the man replies, "How can I, unless someone guides me?" (8:31) It is a classic description of mentors. How can you grow in the faith unless someone guides you, someone older in the faith, wiser, more experienced, even if the guidance is cut tragically short?

Being mentors in the faith is what the priesthood of all believers means. You are called to become what Paul became. But it may not happen until you feel forgiven by a messenger from God whom you first resisted and then attacked.

28

CALLS COME IN
DREAMS
Joseph & Jacob

Many would say that one of the least likely places in which to hear
God speak is in dreams. How can we hear God when we can't
even hear?

We tend to forget that a dream was a listening point for Abraham when
he heard God tell him of the future captivity of the Israelites in Egypt and
their subsequent return to the Promised Land (Gen 15:12-14). It was a
listening point for Jacob when he struggled with God on the banks of the
Jabbok River (Gen 32:24-30). It was a listening point for Joseph, the father
of Jesus, when he was told in a dream to flee to Egypt so the infant Jesus
would not be killed by Herod (Mt 2:13). Dreams are found in the Bible
because they were considered a mode of divine communication. We would
be rash indeed to write them off as merely the result of something we ate.

Dreams Are Elemental
Dreams are a force of nature. According to the scientific evidence, we all
have three to five dreams a night. We may not remember them, but we
all have them. It is not surprising, then, that they should appear frequently
in the Bible.

One reason we do not take them seriously is that they are not something we do. They are beyond us, out of our control. We do not control them; they control us, at least to the extent that they occur without our conscious manipulation.

Since time immemorial, dreams have been interpreted as a way God speaks. Then came Descartes, who reduced life and God to what could be thought "clearly and distinctly." If it wasn't rational, it wasn't real. But dreams are highly irrational and stunningly real. A psychologist has defined them as "sleep think." To cut them out of our thinking is to be out of touch with reality. And to deny they can be revealers of God is at best to be historically naive and at worst theologically illiterate.

Dreams Are Unpredictable

Dreams are also unpredictable. We have no idea where they come from or what they mean.

Joseph dreams that he and his brothers are binding sheaves in the field and that their sheaves bow down to his (Gen 37:5-8). It was a dream as unpredictable as the wind. But he does one crucial thing to lock his dream into consciousness: he shares it. He tells it to his brothers and father. Sharing our dreams every morning, a writer on dreams has said, is surely as instructive as sharing the messages on the shredded wheat box.

The elemental, unpredictable side of our human nature is not easily understood, and if we, as good Cartesian rationalists, reduce life to what can be understood, then we will have missed out on much of life. Indeed, we will have missed out on God, who cannot, by definition, be fully understood. "Life in this family," writes a commentator on the family of Joseph, "will not be reduced to what can be understood."[1]

Dreams have a life of their own. You cannot predict where they will take you or who will go with you. All you need to do is to share them, write them down, lock them into consciousness—and then be surprised, as Joseph was, that your dream was God calling. When asked to interpret the pharaoh's dream, Joseph says, "Do not interpretations belong to God?" (40:8).

Dreams Are Accessible

Elemental, unpredictable, dreams are also accessible. All we have to do is tell ourselves, before going to sleep, that we want to remember them. Then in the morning we can jot down any that affected us emotionally and ask for comments and questions at breakfast. Do not be upset or embarrassed if the dream is negative. Not only do we have three to five dreams a night, it has also been empirically demonstrated that sixty percent of our dreams are negative. However, as we have seen with our troubling emotions, our troubling dreams can be singularly helpful in revealing and releasing the inner self.

Needless to say, there is some risk in sharing your dreams, but the potential reward of God's calling you through your dreams outweighs the risk of going public with them to your family. Joseph's father, for instance, writes Joseph's dream off as absurd. "What is this dream that you have dreamed?" he asks. "Shall I and your mother and your brothers indeed come to bow ourselves to the ground before you?" (Gen 37:10)

The one thing we should not do is write off someone's dream, even our own, as absurd. Most dreams are bizarre, but that does not mean they are absurd or without meaning. A dream may be the most meaningful thing that happens to us in a given day, particularly when it is viewed, as Carl Jung suggested, as an attempt by the unconscious mind to compensate for the day's failures of the conscious mind.

Fortunately, Joseph's father has second thoughts. A dream can obtrude itself onto your consciousness and then linger. "His father kept the saying in mind" (37:11). Far from being dismissed as absurd, the dream forces itself upon him. He cannot stop thinking about it.

Joseph's brothers hate him for his dream and want to kill him. It is the first dream in the Bible about political power. The reason the prophets of Israel got in trouble was that they took the social dimension of their dreams with the utmost seriousness. "If there is a prophet among you," God says to Aaron and Miriam, "I the LORD make myself known to him in a vision, I speak with him in a dream" (Num 12:6).

Later Joseph interprets dreams for the pharaoh's staff and then for the pharaoh himself, giving credit to God for the ability to interpret. "It is not in me," he says. "God will give Pharaoh a favorable answer" (Gen 41:16). He points out that God is speaking to the pharaoh through his dream. "God has revealed to Pharaoh what he is about to do" (41:25).

Dreams Are One-Third of Life

I had never been exposed to the possibilities in dreams until I found myself responding to a brochure about a conference in the Pocono Mountains on spiritual development. The first evening session happened to be on dreams. I was surprised, to say the least, and thought I had wasted my money by going to the wrong conference.

"You'll have your first dream ninety minutes after you go to sleep," the speaker said. Sure enough, at 1:30 a.m. I was awake and writing down a dream, having gone to bed at midnight. I can still remember that dream twenty years later. It was about a depressed downtown area that was in obvious need of renewal. It clearly referred to the renewal that was going on in my life at the time, and, remarkably, I was about to find myself helping to renew a depressed downtown area.

Dreams are perhaps our greatest unexplored resource for hearing the call of God. There probably is not one family in 100,000 that discusses dreams. Families will pray and read the Bible, and individual family members will join small groups to pray and read the Bible and discuss how the Bible relates to their lives. But only rarely will anyone ever bring a dream to those discussion groups.

Every night of your life is a potential listening point. But in spite of all the evidence in the Bible, it may be that the only way we are ever going to know that is for someone to tell us—in an unguarded moment, perhaps, when we are far away from our usual surroundings, as I was in the Poconos, and willing to try anything.

I had recently arrived at a new church as its pastor, and the timing seemed right for learning more about spiritual development. Time and events, nothing more than living out my life, had brought me into an entirely new dimension of reality—how God is speaking to us through the unconscious.

It has now become a mystery to me why the life of the unconscious is not taught in schools and churches. Beginning in the early grades, children could be encouraged to share their dreams with their parents. We give our children incredibly short shrift by eliminating an entire segment of their lives, eight hours out of every twenty-four. It makes no sense. But it probably happens because we are afraid of our dreams, and we are afraid because we are not in control of them.

The unconscious scares us because when we are unconscious we are totally passive—which means, of course, that we are in an ideal place to hear a call. But we do not know that in advance. Being unconscious scares us because we are not in charge—which means, of course, that we are in an ideal place to hear from God who is in charge.

Dreams scare us because the outer self has been put to sleep, the self that deals with paying the mortgage and getting the kids off to school. That self we can deal with. That self we can control. But when we lose control for eight hours a night, the inner self emerges of its own accord, and we are terrified. But in the terror is God, the "fear" of God.

That is why we need, from an early age, to be tutored in how to let God be God. Or, if that is too religious for the schools, let the divine aspect of the unconscious be taught by churches and temples while schools teach the value of dreams in other, secular ways.

At the very least, let us begin sharing our dreams in our homes, trying on different interpretations with each other, and making the assumption that God is doing the interpreting through us and that the dream itself, as happens so often in the Bible, is God calling, just as God called the prophets and Joseph and Jacob and others centuries ago. If it worked for them, why not for us?

JACOB

How do you access your inner self? You don't. It accesses you. One way is through dreams, as Jacob was to discover. He wrestled all night with an angel on the bank of the Jabbok River. As morning breaks he finds himself saying, "I have seen God face to face" (Gen 32:30).

God sees through to the inner Jacob. The inner self, the image of God, is the self God sees. It is hidden from our view because the outer self, with its many accomplishments, obscures the inner self. So layer after layer of the outer self has to be peeled off. Time and events do the peeling, making us ever more accessible to God.

You Find Yourself in Awe
Jacob could do nothing about releasing the inner Jacob. He just went about

his life. At the moment he was fleeing his brother's wrath after stealing his father's blessing. Suddenly God appears, unsolicited, in a dream about a ladder reaching up to heaven (Gen 28:10-17). The ladder was probably a ziggurat, a short pyramid with steps, on which Jacob saw angels ascending and descending.

"And behold, the LORD stood above it and said, 'I am the LORD' " (28:13). God proceeds to call Jacob with the promise that the land on which he is sleeping will be his forever. More than that, the call includes an astonishing vote of confidence in a thief: "Behold, I am with you and will keep you wherever you go" (28:15).

Jacob is understandably awestruck. "How awesome is this place!" he cries (28:17). You know it's a call, or at least could be a call, if you experience awe. It is in his cry of awe—verse 17 also calls it fear—that Jacob is given access to his inner self. "All philosophy begins in wonder," Plato wrote in his *Timaeus* (2e), and religion, the idea that something more than self is there, begins in awe, an emotion that has a tinge of fear, which is why the Bible often speaks of the "fear" of God.

It was for reasons of awe, among others, that Pope John Paul II traveled to the Ivory Coast to dedicate the world's largest church. Incredibly, the church has a dome twice the size of St. Peter's in Rome. The whole point was to create the emotion of awe. That is why church architects make ceilings high. They want to dwarf the worshipers, to emphasize their smallness in the face of God's vastness, and thus create awe.

Remember your awe at the birth of your child or a child close to you? All experiences of awe have the potential to become listening points. Is it any wonder that young parents often begin going to church after the birth of their first child?

You Find Yourself Praying

After his dream, Jacob goes on with his life. He works seven years for Laban to get Rachel as his wife. Instead he gets Leah and has to work another seven to get Rachel. After that he works for Laban another six years. Then he leaves to return home.

On the way, he is met by "the angels of God," so many that he calls them "God's army" (Gen 32:1-2). The point the Bible is making is that God is there for Jacob, again and again, even though Jacob may not be there for God. There is no indication in any of these chapters that Jacob takes any initiative with God. It is all God and no Jacob.

God is constantly there for you even though you may not be there for God. God arrives time after time, unsolicited. It is these gratuitous arrivals in the events of life that gradually increase your awe to the point where, in the fullness of time, you arrive at a listening point.

Indeed, for the first time in eight chapters about Jacob, we find him praying (32:9). It is twenty years since he left home. You may be thirty-eight years old before you find yourself praying, twenty years after you leave home. It may take that long for you to arrive at a listening point. This is all right; remember, it takes whatever it takes to hear a call.

The brash, conniving, arrogant Jacob finds himself, in response to God's repeated initiatives, praying, "O God . . . I am not worthy of the least of all the steadfast love and all the faithfulness which thou hast shown to thy servant" (32:9-10). Humility has begun to set in, another sign of a possible call. The accomplishments of the outer self are being put in perspective so that at last he can "see through" them to his emerging inner self, which is slowly coming into view.

Jacob is to meet his brother Esau the next day, the one whose birthright and blessing he had stolen. "I fear him," he says in his prayer, as well he might (32:11). Indeed, it is his fear that is driving him to prayer, alone there on the banks of the river Jabbok.

Time and events are doing their work, bringing Jacob within hearing distance of God. He is being prepared for one of the most striking direct experiences of God in the Bible, an experience he could not have had twenty years before because he was not ready; he had not *been readied* by the events of his life.

You Find Yourself Wrestling with God

Jacob takes his family across the stream and is left alone, at which point "a man wrestled with him until the breaking of the day" (Gen 32:24). He has been moved from prayer to, possibly, another dream.[2] His assailant is God, wrestling with him to wrest control of his life, so that at last he will live from the inside instead of from the outside. The wrestling match is a dramatic symbol of how, when layer after layer of the outer self has been peeled away by events and we are face to face with the inner self, it is still a struggle for the inner self to assert itself and dominate the outer.

Crossing the river, which Jacob has done, is an ancient symbol of overcoming an obstacle and going forward to a new experience. Julius Caesar's crossing the Rubicon, from which there was no turning back, precipitated a war. There is no turning back now for Jacob in the grip of his adversary. It is a watershed experience. He has to come to grips with his past and what he has done to his brother if he is to go forward to new life.

Who is this adversary? It was thought that rivers were infested by demons. (Remember the story of the troll under the bridge with the billy goats crossing overhead?) Jacob does not know who his adversary is at first. In the same way, we cannot identify our adversary in the heat of a struggle. Is it a demon or an angel? Is it Satan or God? The struggle is at night, when demons are abroad. Our resistance is lowest at night. We toss and turn in our beds. We are alone. We are in the dark about something.

Jacob's adversary is God in the form of a man (Gen 32:24). "I have seen God face to face," Jacob says (32:30). Jacob's dark side, his shadow side, the conniving, deceiving, lying, stealing aspect of his outer self is being subdued in the titanic wrestling match. The dark, outer Jacob loses. As a symbol of his defeat he is given a limp. He becomes helpless with a disjointed thigh. He can no longer wrestle. God has won. The inner self has been brought to light. Day dawns.

We have to suffer to be whole, to hear the call of God evoking the inner self. The events of life bring suffering, sometimes of our own making. Suffering brings awe. Awe brings God. The flawed hero leaves home. He works at hard labor for twenty years. Then he returns home, but not without still more suffering, symbolized in the Jacob story by the disjointed thigh.

You Find Your Inner Self Revealed

Often, the hero is given a new name as a symbol of his new self. "Your name shall no more be called Jacob," his adversary tells him, "but Israel, for you have striven with God and with men, and have prevailed" (Gen 32:28). The name *Israel* means "One who strives with God" or "God strives." The same thing happened to Paul, who had been called Saul, Peter who had been called Cephas. It is what happens in a baptism, when a name is given and the congregation prays that the child will live up to his or her Christian name, thus becoming a new person in Christ, a "new creation" (2 Cor 5:17).

Dawn breaks. Demons vanish with the light. So the adversary says to Jacob, "Let me go, for the day is breaking" (Gen 32:26). The return of light signifies how Jacob now sees himself in a new light, and it is now, at the dawn, that his adversary gives him the blessing of a new name. He has been called to new life. He is a new Jacob. God has descended the ladder of his dream and wrestled with him for his soul. And God has won.

Jacob goes to his brother limping—humble, repentant, no longer striding, arrogant. And what does his brother do on seeing him? "Esau ran to meet him, and embraced him, and fell on his neck and kissed him, and they wept" (33:4).

But would it have happened if he had not found himself dreaming, praying and suffering, if God had not been searching out his soul? His inner self, as he did nothing more than live out his life, had been revealed.

Part VI

WHY IS A CALL
NOT HEARD?

29

CALLS ARE NOT HEARD
BECAUSE OF GREED

Solomon

Solomon is the classic example of how greed can deafen us to a call. He who had raised his hand to God at the dedication of the temple would soon have it said of him, "His heart was not wholly true to the LORD his God" (1 Kings 11:4). What went wrong?

Love of Money Can Deafen You to a Call

For one thing, Solomon put his economics ahead of his theology, his greed ahead of his God. It is a temptation for all of us. A good case can be made that economics rules the world. Civilizations follow the trade routes. America was settled by people who, among other things, wanted to make money. We go wherever we can make the most. So do nations.

Solomon loved his money. He built the temple in Jerusalem, and then he built a palace even larger. He treatied and married his way from Egypt to Mesopotamia, which meant that he controlled all the trade routes in the Middle East and so was able to exact exorbitant tolls for their use.

His interest in the fabled Queen of Sheba was solely for economic reasons. He needed her for products and trade routes; she needed him for northern ports to market her goods. His ships would be gone for three years at a time, bringing back luxuries for him to sell at huge profits—gold, silver, ivory, apes, peacocks (1 Kings 10:22).

None of this economic activity was without its benefits, of course, even if it progressively diverted its chief architect from God. There was a certain Pax Hebraica from Egypt to Mesopotamia and north to Syria. It was the kingdom that his father, David, had established and that he, as an executive and economist par excellence, was to continue and enhance. He preceded Alexander the Great and the Pax Hellenica by six hundred years and was the precursor of an even wider-ranging Pax Romana at the time of Jesus.

Solomon's great contribution was that he saw that international peace was necessary for economic prosperity. "The requirements of the Solomonic age," writes a scholar, "led to the first known formulation of international peace—'Nation shall not lift up sword against nation, neither shall they learn war any more' " (Mic 4:3).[1] That formulation is inscribed in the plaza across from the United Nations building in New York City.

All, however, was not sweetness and light. Our greatest ability can also be our greatest vulnerability. Solomon's economic policies were eventually ruinous. "When he died," writes historian Will Durant, "Israel was exhausted."[2]

To build his temple and palace and fortify his cities, Solomon had to resort to forced labor. To pay off his debts, he had to mortgage his northern cities. To stave off economic disaster, he had to levy burdensome taxes on eleven of his twelve administrative districts, the twelfth, his own, remaining untaxed. As the deficit grew, so did the unrest, and after a while it was only a matter of time before the consequences would be dire. Indeed, it was under Solomon that class warfare in Israel began, with rich against poor.[3]

Solomon was so rich and powerful he didn't need God. "His heart was not wholly true to the Lord his God." And yet, as with Saul, everything had started off well. "Solomon loved the LORD," we read (1 Kings 3:3). "I am but a little child," he says to God at an early listening point (3:7).

We love our money too much. It is foremost in our thoughts. We are constantly concerned about salary, car payments, college payments, retirement account payments, a new TV, cellular phone, microwave. The list is endless. We think more about money than we think about God.

Your Spouse Can Deafen You to a Call

In the course of accumulating his riches, Solomon also accumulated seven hundred wives and three hundred concubines, although they may have been only sixty and eighty respectively, according to some scholars. In either case, they were a sign of munificence rather than concupiscence. The Bible writer uses Solomon's wives to explain his downfall. "His wives turned away his heart" (1 Kings 11:3).

Many of Solomon's wives were foreigners. In those days a head of state would marry to insure a trade relationship with another state. Solomon readily built his wives shrines for their gods. He even put their shrines on top of the Mount of Olives, thus causing it to be called the Mount of Corruption (2 Kings 23:13).

The writer reports that "Solomon went after Ashtoreth the goddess of the Sidonians, and after Milcom the abomination of the Ammonites" (1 Kings 11:5). Ashtoreth was the principal Phoenician goddess, symbolized by the moon. Solomon needed Phoenicia for his ships and timber. Do you see how easily the economic subverts the religious? Milcom was the god of the Ammonites, who lived due east of Israel. Solomon needed Ammon to protect his eastern flank.

Cases are legion in which one spouse will let the other determine the couple's religion. The one spouse becomes Solomonic in his or her obsession with making money at work or in the stock market or simply keeping track of the family finances. He or she becomes as deaf to a call as Solomon and is unconcerned about the other spouse's religion.

"Thou shalt have no other gods before me" was the call (Ex 20:3). But Solomon was no longer at a listening point. He had fallen away from obeying the call he had heard through his dying father to "keep the charge of the LORD your God" (1 Kings 2:3), and now was inured to future calls. It could happen to any of us.

You Find Yourself Answering the Call

What is the answer? The answer is not to let the economic usurp the religious. How do we do that? We don't. Only God can.

"Seek first his kingdom and his righteousness," calls Jesus, "and all these things shall be yours as well" (Mt 6:33). It is an impossible command. Human nature isn't up to obeying it. But "What is impossible for mortals," Jesus also said, "is possible for God" (Lk 18:27 NRSV). In the impossibility is the call.

When we find ourselves thinking as much about God as we do about money, that is God. When we find ourselves tithing, as the Word of God commands (Deut 14:22), that is God. We are at a listening point when we find ourselves buying the new microwave for the homeless shelter as well as one for ourselves.

What can we do to accomplish such laudable objectives? Nothing. The events of life will eventually bring us to their accomplishment. And if they don't, then they don't, just as they didn't for Solomon. It is too bad, but that is the way it is sometimes.

But don't we have control over the events of life? Of course, to some extent, although there are always the calamities that happen beyond our control, such as illness, hurricane, death. It is the sum total of events we do control and those we do not that will eventually enable us to hear God's call to "keep the charge of the LORD your God."

But what about those events we do control? If they were part of getting us to hear God call, can't we take at least partial credit for hearing a call? No we can't, because they were simply how we were living out our lives, putting one foot in front of the other, with no thought of God—going to work, coming home, watching TV, putting the kids to bed. And if we did have a thought of God and, say, found ourselves praying with our children as we put them to bed, that was God, not us. The credit has to be God's; it cannot be ours, or the religious game is up, as we saw in part one.

"No one can come to me," we recall Jesus saying, "unless drawn by the Father who sent me" (Jn 6:44 NRSV). "You did not choose me, but I chose you" (Jn 15:16). "No one can say 'Jesus is Lord,' " Paul wrote, "except by the Holy Spirit" (1 Cor 12:3).

Paul puts the matter of choice in perspective. "Christ Jesus has made me his own," he writes (Phil 3:12). "I have been crucified with Christ; it is no longer I who live but Christ who lives in me" (Gal 2:20). And in Ephesians we read, "For by grace you have been saved through faith, and this is not your own doing; it is the gift of God—not the result of works, so that no one may boast" (2:8-9 NRSV).

The idea that calls are all God's work and not ours goes back to the beginning. "The LORD has chosen you," the Bible says (Deut 14:2). It does not say, "You have chosen the Lord." Remember, a call is passive, never active.

To be sure, the Bible often suggests that we can choose God. "Choose this day whom you will serve," Joshua says to the nation, "but as for me and my house, we will serve the LORD" (Josh 24:15). Just as mercy beats judgment in the Bible and unconditional love beats conditional, so passive beats active, *chosen* beats *choose*.

In point of fact, the Israelites rarely chose the Lord. They were always choosing otherwise, as the story of Solomon vividly attests. They were the chosen people, not the choosing people. And whenever they did choose the Lord, the power of the Lord was enabling them to choose.

> I will heal their faithlessness;
> I will love them freely, . . .
> I will be as the dew to Israel;
> he shall blossom as the lily,
> he shall strike root as the poplar. . . .
> I am like an evergreen cypress,
> from me comes your fruit. (Hos 14:4-5, 8)

Solomon was clearly at odds with his religious tradition when he let his affluence get in the way of his God. His tradition was clear, going back to Moses and the Deuteronomic Code: "Beware lest you say in your heart, 'My power and the might of my hand have gotten me this wealth.' You shall remember the LORD your God, for it is he who gives you power to get wealth. . . . And if you forget the LORD your God and go after other gods and serve them and worship them, I solemnly warn you this day that you shall surely perish" (Deut 8:17-19). Solomon forgot. And perished.

We can boast about nothing when it comes to hearing our calls or obeying them. We can take zero credit. That is what makes them calls and not achievements. Solomon's problem was that his achievements had deafened him to his calls.

30

CALLS ARE NOT HEARD
BECAUSE OF
SELF-RELIANCE

The Rich Young Ruler

The rich young ruler appeared to be an ideal listener. He had everything going for him. He was the first century's equivalent of an MBA, one of the best and brightest, a clear winner. In addition, he felt something was still missing in his life, and he had been drawn to Jesus to find it.

Indeed, the rich young ruler was such a winner that he ran to Jesus, knelt before him in a gesture of reverence and humility, and then, in answer to a question from Jesus, told him that he had kept all the commandments—no mean feat for anyone. No wonder the Bible says that Jesus "looking upon him loved him" (Mk 10:21). It has even been suggested that Jesus wanted him as his thirteenth disciple.

Your Control of Events Can Deafen You to a Call

The rich young ruler comes to Jesus out of his need. "What is still missing in my life?" he asks (Mt 19:20 Phillips). There was a void, an emptiness. He had accomplished much, but he had much more to accomplish. He had kept all the commandments, done all the right things, been to the right schools, gotten the best conceivable start in life, and yet something was missing. He may have looked as though he had everything going for him, but he knew in his heart he did not.

Jesus calls us when we have a hunch that he can supply what is missing in life. Specifically, the rich young ruler was missing an answer to the question, "What good deed must I do, to have eternal life?" (Mt 19:16) He had had everything up to that point, so why not go for the ultimate, eternal life? Everything had come his way in temporal life, so why not eternal as well? Life has been so good to us we want it to go on forever.

Jesus gives the young man his answer. Keep the Ten Commandments, he tells him. The young man says that he has, and it is at this point that he says he is still missing something. What he is missing, although he does not know it yet, is his "passive" side, which he has lost, as many young people have, by devoting too much attention to his "active" side.

"What must I *do* to inherit eternal life?" He was not yet in touch with his inmost self because Jesus had not yet been able to put him in touch. And Jesus had been unable to put him in touch because the rich young ruler was too young and too rich. Life's events had not caught up with him yet, as they had with Paul. He was still in control of events, as all self-reliant people are, or at least think they are.

The rich young ruler was at that point in life where he was what he did rather than did what he was. But if he could only see that he was a child of God who needed God's help to keep the Ten Commandments, then the doing would take care of itself. "Love God," St. Augustine said, "and do as you please"—as opposed to, "Do all the right things, and then you will love God."

We have the notion that if we can do all the right things, if we can be successful, if we can climb the corporate ladder, raise nice children and have a good marriage, then we can achieve whatever degree of immortality is within our grasp to achieve. As someone said to me once of American life, "Everyone's wound up two turns too tight."

Such an attitude stands in direct contrast to the one Jesus suggests. You *are* a success, he says; you don't have to *become* a success. You are a success because you are a child of God. You don't have to earn your way. You don't have to do anything to get right with God. To prove his point he gives the young man just what he needs, an impossible order, something he can't do on his own. "If you would be perfect," he says, with possible irony, "sell what you possess and give to the poor, and you will have treasure in heaven; and come, follow me" (Mt 19:21).

He couldn't do it. That was the point. It would have to be all God and no rich young ruler. Thinking he could do anything, the young man came to Jesus. But Jesus made him realize there was something he couldn't do, in order to tap in to his inmost self. This meant getting the young man off his self-reliance. "The ending of our lives would not threaten us," Reinhold Niebuhr wrote, "if we had not falsely made ourselves the center of life's meaning."

If you want to find what you are missing in life, Jesus is saying, if you want the eternal life you have come to me for, then try something impossible, something beyond your vaunted ability, and something that will help other people. That is how you will become the thirteenth disciple—when you are thrown off your own resources and onto God's, because it is only then that your "being" as a child of God will catch up to your "doing" as a young MBA-type who can do anything.

But the young man cannot hear the call. It falls on deaf ears. "His countenance fell," the Bible says in a memorable sentence, "and he went away sorrowful; for he had great possessions" (Mk 10:22).

Your Needs Can Deafen You to a Call

What went wrong? Why wasn't he up to it? Why did one of the most promising listening points in the Bible turn out not to be one after all? The answer can only be that the rich young ruler's need wasn't deep enough. His question—"What is still missing in my life?"—must have been academic only, intellectual but not yet visceral. He was needy, all right, but he wasn't needy enough. His need wasn't yet a hunger. He was too self-reliant. He could still meet all his needs himself.

Apparently needs alone are not sufficient to bring us to a listening point. They have to become hungers. We have to hunger for what is missing in life or we will never hear the call of Christ. Do you need peace at home or work so badly it has become a hunger? Then you may be at a listening point. Do you need freedom from anxiety, guilt or failure so badly it has become a hunger? Mary Magdalene was in dire need and hungry for help. The rich young ruler was in intellectual need and not yet hungry for help.

Soon after converting to Quakerism, William Penn went to George Fox, the leading Quaker of the day, and asked him when he, Penn, as a member of the English aristocracy, should stop wearing his sword—Quakers, of course, being pacifists. Fox replied, "When you are ready."

When we are ready our need will have become a hunger. How do you know it's a hunger and not a need? You give it the stomach test. If it's that deep, having gone from your head to your gut, then you're in touch with something that is missing enough in your life to bring you to a listening point.

What distracts you at work or at home so much that you can't concentrate on your family or your job? That's a hunger. The rich young ruler wasn't hungry enough to hear and hence obey Jesus. He wasn't hungry enough to find what he was missing.

Such hungers are involuntary. They are just there. Your hunger for what you are missing in life is not something over which you have any control. Remember, this is your "being," not your "doing." It is the essence of who you are. You cannot will hunger. Hunger just is. You cannot will any control over your hunger, except for a short time at Lent, perhaps, or with a hunger strike. You cannot will away your hunger. And when it comes to spiritual hunger, there is no amount of eating through doing that can eliminate the hunger.

It is perhaps no accident that Christians' most sacred ritual, holy Communion, involves eating. It is Jesus who satisfies our deepest hunger. If Jesus is ever going to call us at a listening point, he will have to come as the spiritual food that satisfies our deepest hunger.

There is an enormous difference between trying to satisfy our own needs and having Jesus satisfy our deepest hungers. It is the difference between being a rich young ruler and a disciple. The disciples heard the call, obeyed by following Jesus, then were so surprised by what they found themselves doing that they knew *they* weren't doing it. "Lord," they exclaim, "even the demons are subject to us in your name!" (Lk 10:17).

By contrast, the rich young ruler, being rich and young and a ruler, was so proud of what he was able to do in life, namely rule and be rich, that he wasn't yet ready for the involuntary side of life, for what could be done through him by God rather than by him as a rich young ruler. That was why Jesus gave him the impossible command, "Sell what you have and give to the poor."

Jesus was always giving impossible commands to self-reliant, can-do types who felt they could do the impossible. He was trying to get them off their own resources and onto God's, off their needs and onto their hungers, off their heads and into their stomachs.

We are surprised by God when we find ourselves obeying any of Jesus' commands. The surprise is that we know it is not we who are obeying them. It is God enabling us to obey. Wherever the story of the rich young ruler appears in the Gospels, it is always followed by Jesus saying, "For mortals it is impossible, but for God all things are possible" (Mt 19:26 NRSV).

One way, then, to hear God calling at a listening point is to feel yourself irresistibly drawn by whatever you may be hungry for in life to the one who said, "I am the bread of life. Whoever comes to me will never be hungry, and whoever believes in me will never be thirsty" (Jn 6:35 NRSV). For that hunger to be felt, you may have to come up against something in life that is too big for self-reliance to handle. Wherever that is, there your listening point can be.

31

CALLS ARE NOT HEARD
BECAUSE OF ILLNESS
Hezekiah

J ust as certain defects of character can deafen us to a call, so can illness. Illness increases vulnerability, and when we are vulnerable we can either rely on God or give up on God.

You Find Yourself Relying on God in a Tough Situation

The story of one of the Bible's most successful kings is instructive. The year is 705 B.C., and Judah is being attacked by Assyria. Hezekiah fights back. "He rebelled against the king of Assyria," the Bible says (2 Kings 18:7). Hezekiah was tough. He had become king ten years earlier at age twenty-five. His performance reviews were excellent. "Wherever he went forth he prospered" (18:7).

Hezekiah was also a listener. The Bible gives him high marks for holding fast to God while holding out against Assyria. "He trusted in the LORD the God of Israel; so that there was none like him among all the kings of Judah after him, nor among those who were before him" (18:5).

One reason Hezekiah was revered was that he destroyed the idols, many of them set up on hills, that had cropped up in Israel's religious practices. He "removed the high places, and broke the pillars, and cut down the Asherah" (18:4). He was as zealous as Solomon had been indifferent. He removed all vestiges of idol worship.

I was talking once with a highly placed friend whose corporation's name is a household word. He was telling me how he could not do his job without God, but if his job were to become his god, he would be an idolater no different from many of the ancient Hebrews on their high places.

Unfortunately for Hezekiah and the populace, Assyria's attack is not repulsed and it soon turns into a siege. Hezekiah is drawn to a listening point. He finds himself in the temple where he can worship and ask for help from the prophet Isaiah. Isaiah assures him that all will be well.

At this point a letter arrives from the enemy. "Do not let your God on whom you rely deceive you," writes Sennacherib (19:10). Hezekiah reads the letter, takes it to the temple and, in a memorable image, spreads it out before the Lord and prays (19:14-19). He is assured that God will "put the hook" in Sennacherib's nose and take him back to Assyria. Indeed, Sennacherib hears a rumor, rushes back and is murdered by his son.

So we have a Hezekiah who has been attacked and then besieged, but who has met his twin challenges as he finds himself listening for God.

You Fail to Rely on God in an Even Tougher Situation

But then Hezekiah is attacked by a new enemy, a fatal illness, and this time he is not so successful. "Thus says the LORD," Isaiah tells him, " 'Set your house in order; for you shall die, you shall not recover' " (2 Kings 20:1).

Hezekiah cannot believe it. He turns his face to the wall and prays. " 'Remember now, O LORD, I beseech thee, how I have walked before thee in faithfulness and with a whole heart, and have done what is good in thy sight.' And Hezekiah wept bitterly" (20:3).

Immediately there is a dramatic turnabout. Isaiah is stopped in the middle of the courtyard and is told by God to go back to Hezekiah and tell him that he has heard his prayer and seen his tears and will give him fifteen more years to live.

It could not be better news, but Hezekiah is suddenly skeptical and asks Isaiah for a sign. He needs proof that he will be healed. So Isaiah asks God to turn back the clock on the sundial, Hezekiah having insisted that it be turned back rather than pushed ahead because pushing it ahead would be too easy. So God brings the shadow on the sundial back ten steps, and Hezekiah's disease is turned back even as his attackers had been turned back (2 Kings 20:8-11).

But at what price? He has put God to the test, the very temptation Jesus avoided in the wilderness (Mt 4:7). His faith was not so faithful after all, not if he needed a sign to serve as a pledge that God would do what God had already said God would do. Of course, Gideon also asked for a sign, got one, was considered faithful and went on to victory (Judg 6:17—17:25).

Your Pride Deafens You to a Call

Hezekiah's devolution continues as he sinks to the nadir of his career and his faith. "There was none like him among all the kings of Judah" (2 Kings 18:5), yet it is he who sells out his country and forsakes his God.

The Babylonians have heard he is sick and use it as an excuse to come to call. What they really want is an alliance with him against Assyria. Isaiah had warned Hezekiah against such an alliance, but Hezekiah justifies it with one of the most cynical and self-serving sentences in the Bible: "Why not, if there will be peace and security in my days?" (20:19). It was the 1938 Munich Agreement 2,600 years earlier.

He then proceeds to show the Babylonians "all that is in my house"— the gold, silver, spices, oils, armory, everything in his storehouse and treasure house (20:13-15). In other words, he has revealed state secrets to a potential enemy. It is one of the most inexplicable reversals in the Bible. It is so appalling that there is a break in the Bible after Isaiah 39, where Isaiah tells about the alliance with Babylon, and Isaiah writes no more. The rest of Isaiah is written by two other people writing from exile in, you guessed it, Babylon, after the fall of Jerusalem in 586 B.C.

What happened? Nobody knows. All we can do is speculate. Perhaps the writer of Chronicles speculates best. "Hezekiah did not make return according to the benefit done to him, for his heart was proud" (2 Chron 32:25). His illness had upset his rhythm of prayer and worship. Then when he was healed, his healing had for some reason thrust him onto his own resources and off God's. It had obstructed his way to any new listening points, the exact opposite of what happened to Naaman and Mary Magdalene.

We pray for help when we need it, and then we forget God. It happens all the time. Once the crisis is past, we are back on our own. What could have been a series of listening points becomes a vanishing point instead. God, of course, has not vanished, but we have vanished from God. When we are well, who needs God? When we are sick and get well, who needs God? When we are sick and don't get well, that's another matter. Then we need God very much. But by then we may be so far from God that we are out of calling distance.

The irony of the Hezekiah story is that for most of his life Hezekiah was very much within calling distance. He went from one listening point to another. He found himself praying and worshiping regularly and hearing from God regularly. Perhaps it has been the same for you. But then when God heals him, he abruptly abandons God. Being well, he has no need of God. The consequences are disastrous.

Count forward seven hundred years to Jesus. "Your king comes to you . . . humble," Zechariah had prophesied (Zech 9:9). Jesus "emptied himself," Paul wrote, "taking the form of a servant" (Phil 2:7). How can we be humble enough to hear God calling in both success and illness?

The answer can only be that we cannot. Only Jesus could. We have to be humbled. Ironically, Hezekiah was able to hear God calling in his humbling vocational challenge, at least at first, but not in his humbling medical challenge. His vocational success, unlike Solomon's and Saul's and the rich young ruler's, had not made him so proud that he could no longer be humble enough to hear God. It is a good example of how positive events can bring us to listening points.

Unfortunately, when events turn negative and Hezekiah is threatened with death, arguably his greatest challenge, his heroic ego reasserts itself and he puts God to the test—a good example of how negative events can turn us away from a listening point. Apparently Hezekiah, unlike Job after his sufferings, had not been sufficiently humbled, even by his near-death experience, to hear God call, which is why the Bible says he "did not make return according to the benefit done to him, for his heart was proud" (2 Chron 32:25). Humility is a problem for kings—and for the king in us.

The answer, then, to hearing God call in the problems of life would appear to be to find ourselves continuing, through even the most devastating problem, to pray and to worship. When we find ourselves doing so, we are at a listening point. It has to be God, it cannot be us, because we are too much like Hezekiah.

But we are not left to be like Hezekiah. That is the message of the Bible. No matter how far we may have strayed out of calling distance, it is always possible that the events of life can bring us to a listening point. They can humble us to the point where we can hear God call.

32

CALLS ARE NOT HEARD
BECAUSE OF SUCCESS

Saul

*S*aul had everything going for him. He was the leader of his country and immensely popular. He had checked the Philistines in the central highlands. He had stopped the Amalekite incursions. He had separated religion and state to an unheard-of degree. He had built an unpretentious capital. He was spiritually gifted; he heard God speak and admitted his faults.

It Is Easy to Get Out of Calling Distance
Then he falls apart. Saul gets out of calling distance. How it happened is anyone's guess. It is the human predicament. Jesus alone was able to stay within calling distance. That is why we need call after call to keep hearing God, which means we need event after event in life to get us back within calling distance.

It seems we can be obedient for a while. A call heard is a call obeyed. But then sin reasserts itself, sin beats grace, the outer self obscures the inner once more, and we begin to drop away from our calls. The dropout rate from calls is alarming.

What had Saul done? How had his divided nature reasserted itself?

How had his ego once again become ascendant over his alter ego?

In going up against the Amalekites, God calls him through Samuel to destroy them. "Do not spare them, but kill both man and woman, child and infant, ox and sheep, camel and donkey" (1 Sam 15:3 NRSV). For some reason the call is not heard. Saul spares Agag the king and keeps the best cattle and sheep for later sacrifice.

Saul's partial obedience sounds reasonable to us, but for not obeying God totally, Samuel is ruthless in his judgment. "You have rejected the word of the LORD," he says, "and the LORD has rejected you from being king over Israel" (15:26). We cannot believe it. For showing a little mercy to the opposition leader and allowing the army to give God the spoils of war, that same God relieves him of his command.

Nor can Saul believe it. "I have sinned," he admits. "I have transgressed. . . . Now therefore, I pray, pardon my sin" (15:24-25). But Samuel will have none of it. In desperation Saul, who is already on his knees, grabs Samuel by the hem of his robe and the robe tears. Unfeeling and unyielding, Samuel says, "The LORD has torn the kingdom of Israel from you this day, and has given it to a neighbor of yours, who is better than you" (15:28). There is none of the redemption that often tempers retribution elsewhere in the Bible.

What is going on? It seems as arbitrary as what happened to Moses when he was forbidden, for some undisclosed sin, to enter the Promised Land. The only hint we have of Moses' transgression is at the waters of Meribah in the wilderness of Zin, where God tells Moses to speak to the rock and it will produce water for the people. Instead, Moses takes his rod and strikes the rock. Retribution is as quick and terrible as it was for Saul. "Ascend this mountain," God says, ". . . and die on the mountain which you ascend . . . because you broke faith with me in the midst of the people of Israel at the waters of Meri-bath-kadesh, in the wilderness of Zin" (Deut 32:49-51). After leading the people out of Egypt and through the wilderness, Moses is denied access to the Promised Land.

How to Tell When You Are Getting Out of Calling Distance

Regardless of the situation, the fact is that Saul does not hear the call he is supposed to hear. Had he heard it, he would have obeyed it. Somehow, possibly because he was so successful, he had gotten out of calling distance and events had not yet brought him back.

We may not like what Saul was asked to obey, but that is irrelevant. We must beware of thinking anachronistically. Standards of justice and mercy were clearly different in 1000 B.C. The point the Bible is making is that the consequences of getting out of calling distance can be calamitous.

How can you tell when you are out of calling distance? When you catch yourself blaming others for what you have done. "The people took of the spoil," Saul says (1 Sam 15:21). He blames the people rather than accepting responsibility himself as their leader. Thus he escalates his offense.

We also become deaf to a call when we are jealous. Saul is so jealous of David, the neighbor who was better than he, that he wants to eliminate him as a rival. He tries to pin him to the wall with his spear. He tries to get his own son to kill him. He sends his police to kill him while he is asleep. He turns David's own bodyguard against him. He murders the priest of Nob who had unwittingly assisted David.

Saul pursues David to Horesh, Engedi and the wilderness of Ziph, where David and Abishai steal upon him at night and take his spear and water jug, thus announcing they could have killed him (26:6-12). After that, Saul, to his credit, acknowledges his sin in trying to kill David (26:21), but how much better if he had acknowledged it at the first twinge of jealousy.

We also get out of calling distance when we think more highly of ourselves than of God. There is a little-remembered vignette of the fall of Saul in which Samuel receives word from God to go to Saul and confront him about his getting out of calling distance. On the way he is given directions by the locals: "Saul came to Carmel," they tell Samuel, "and behold, he set up a monument for himself and turned, and passed on, and went down to Gilgal" (15:12). He had set up a monument to himself rather than to God.

To be sure, erecting a monument after a victory was a typical practice in those days. But self-glorification can easily lead to a repeat of the grandiosity of the tower of Babel. "Come," the builders say, "let us make a name for ourselves" (Gen 11:4). Realizing this, God says, perhaps ironically, "Nothing that they propose to do will now be impossible for them" (11:6).

But a call *is* impossible. That is what makes it a call. A call is not something we can obey on our own. When we begin to make monuments to ourselves and put our degrees on our walls and become locally famous for what we have accomplished in life, that is when we are most in danger of getting out of calling distance and not arriving at a listening point.

Why? Because we can do it. Nothing is impossible for us. We don't need God's help. And we certainly don't need God's helper to remind us that life has its listening points, where what is to be done will be done through us rather than by us. Success has an alarming tendency to deafen us to our calls. That is why Martin Luther, who had his own challenges with success as the founder of the Reformation, would say, "He who undertakes anything without a divine call seeks his own glory."

Hopefully, you will find yourself keeping in touch with the one who has anointed you, who has helped you to hear God's call. It could be your spouse, your child, your parent, your pastor, your friend—the person who can remind you that you are in danger of missing a listening point whenever you blame or are jealous or proud.

If Saul had stayed close to Samuel, who had anointed him king, he might never have consulted the witch of Endor. Here is the king, the father of his country, the first monarch in its history, such a good ruler that he was never confronted with a serious rebellion the way David would be, consulting a witch to conjure up the ghost of Samuel so that the prophet can tell him what God is calling him to do.

"Bring up Samuel for me," he pleads with the witch (1 Sam 28:11), in a desperate search for a listening point, forgetting that we cannot conjure our listening points, we can only arrive at them once we have been brought by the events of life. But when Samuel appears, all Samuel can say is to repeat what he had said before: Because Saul turned from God, God has now turned from Saul. The next day Saul falls on his sword at the battle of Mt. Gilboa.

You Find Yourself Giving All the Credit to God for Your Success
The fall of Saul is particularly tragic because he had been on the right

track up to the point of his disobeying Samuel. He had been so inspired by an earlier call that his inspiration had become proverbial: "Is Saul also among the prophets?" (1 Sam 10:12). This was an idiom for saying he was an inspired man of God. When he was anointed king, Samuel said to him, "The spirit of the Lord will come mightily upon you, and you . . . [will] be turned into another man" (10:6).

Saul's inspiration was proof of the transforming power of his listening points. It was this transformation Jesus talked about with Nicodemus when he told him he needed to be "born anew" (Jn 3:3). Even at the end of his life, Saul turns to the Lord in prayer and only consults the witch of Endor when "the LORD did not answer him" (1 Sam 28:6).

Somewhere along the line Saul got off the track. Was it because he was too busy building monuments to his success? Because he was jealous? Because he would not accept responsibility for his actions?

If you find yourself giving credit to God for whatever success you may have in life, and if you find yourself not needing to compare yourself to anyone else, and if you find yourself taking responsibility for your actions, then you may well find yourself within calling distance and, once again, hearing the call of God.

CONCLUSION

This has been a book about the two aspects of the self. We are split between the outer and the inner self, between the self that carries on the day-to-day activities of life and the "inmost self" Paul identified and which the book of Genesis calls the "image of God."

This split is known as sin, and the healing of the split is known as salvation. The way to salvation is through religion, being "bound back" (from the root for *religion*) to the rest of who we are—an inner as well as an outer self. The way of salvation is the way of wholeness (*salvation* coming from the root for "whole").

Our religious tradition is particularly helpful in bringing us wholeness. It is the religion of the "people of the Book," Jews and Christians. The Book contains stories of plain, average, ordinary men and women who found salvation. They discovered healing as the call of God interdicted the sinful spiral of their lives. And they were surprised by a wholeness they had never known as they found themselves doing things they had never dreamed they could.

One particularly compelling story in this Book is of a man who, in his own person, is able to atone for the sin of everyone. His life, death and resurrection put people "at one" with themselves, with others, and with God as he obeys the call of God to "atone" for their sins. He is the only one in the Book who moves from listening point to listening point obeying his call each time.

We Do All That We Can to Heal Our Split

Of course, many of us feel we can do without the Book and can achieve all the wholeness we ever wanted or needed on our own. So we do all that we can to bind ourselves back together. "Work out your own salvation with fear and trembling," Paul wrote (Phil 2:12). We pull out all the stops, including all the pop-psychology self-help books we can lay our hands on. We may even go to a therapist to become what we feel we were meant to be. Such measures may be helpful, make no mistake. But they invariably fall short. We still feel uneasy about ourselves.

If we think we can will our way to unity, we are back with the Pharisees of old. By following the 613 self-help rules of their religion, the Pharisees operated under the mistaken notion that they could will their way to salvation. It can't be done, as Paul the Pharisee was to discover.

There are plenty of contemporary pharisees who feel they can achieve their own salvation. From so-called "positive thinkers" to "possibility thinkers" to "positive mental attitude" practitioners, their numbers are legion. They are the heirs of Emerson's cult of self-reliance, which was itself an heir of that old heretic Pelagius, a fifth-century monk who taught that you could will your way to God. It can't be done. If it could, then God would not be God.

What we discover after trying all the self-help measures at our disposal is that they can get us only so far. In order to get farther, in order to have our split personality healed, in order to be "saved" in religious language, we need outside help. We need something outside us to get inside us and barrel us over the continental divide in ourselves. Proof of our inability to do so on our own is that we are still restless, still uneasy, still frustrated in our attempts to be the person we could be and know we should be.

We Discover That We Need Help to Heal Our Split

Enter religion and the power of God to merge the inner and the outer selves. God does what we cannot do. Proof is the people in the Bible who became what they were capable of becoming when God called them, but

CONCLUSION

who had been incapable of reaching their full potential on their own.

Proof is also here and now in our own lives as we find ourselves becoming who we really are. How do we know we, too, are being called? Because we feel we are at a listening point, where everything comes together, and we feel the "love, joy, and peace," Paul the ex-Pharisee talked about. We feel we can take on the world. Life has meaning and purpose. Many of the good things we yearned for now begin to happen.

Consequently, this book has been an attempt to call psychology back to its religious roots. The word *psychology* comes from the Greek for "study of the soul," and what psychology has forgotten, or deliberately neglected, is the very thing it is supposedly meant to be studying, namely, the soul.

The soul is what Paul called the inmost self and what the writer of Genesis called the image of God. The inmost self becomes united with the outer self in the religious process known as a call. The resulting unity gives us a self that is at home with itself, in harmony with itself, at one with itself—at least for the moment.

What is usually forgotten about Paul's injunction to "work out your own salvation with fear and trembling" is the rest of the sentence: "for God is at work in you, both to will and to work for his good pleasure" (Phil 2:13). It is the power of God that binds our separate selves back together and makes us whole, with the result that we are happy, fulfilled, energized, at peace with who we are and with the world around us.

It is, however, just this action of God that is hard for good old can-do individualists to swallow. We are in the habit of doing everything we can to find happiness on our own. We spend much of our lives stretching the muscles of the ego, and it is not until an appropriate amount of time and events have occurred in life that we realize we cannot find the happiness we seek on our own. We need to have help.

Eventually We Arrive at a Listening Point

The good news of the gospel is that help is there—in the Bible in the lives of plain, average, ordinary people like us who, as someone put it, were "snatched from the banality of their lives" and became the models of faith we need to show us the way to wholeness. Many of them, too, had pulled out all the stops. They had searched everywhere for meaning, purpose, fulfillment and happiness as they lived out their lives like the rest of us.

What the very human beings in the Bible were amazed to discover was that meaning, purpose, fulfillment and happiness had been searching for them all along, and would finally find them in the form of a messenger from God. Indeed, the feeling they eventually were to have that life was meaningful, purposeful, fulfilled and happy, was God.

Who are such messengers? For Moses it was a burning bush, for Deborah a palm tree, for Joseph a dream, for Philemon a friend. God can turn anybody or anything into a listening point at the right time in your life. We call such events *crises,* from the Greek for "turning point."

A crisis can be either positive or negative. It doesn't matter. What does matter is that the turning point will not be viewed as a listening point unless time and events have done their work and we are sensitized at last to the possibility of something more in life, namely, God. All turning points, therefore, are not necessarily listening points, but all listening points will be turning points.

The unpredictability of our crises is why we can say that it takes whatever it takes to bring us to God. You can't legislate. You can't prescribe. Everyone is different. It is why we can also say that all you need to do to "find God" is do what you are already doing. Then you will be found. Simply live out your life and you will be brought to your listening points.

Your first listening point could well come when you fall in love, a positive crisis if ever there was one. Falling in love is completely beyond your control. That is why it is called "falling." There isn't an ounce of will in it. It is beyond choice, beyond will, beyond decision. You don't choose to fall in love. You don't decide. You fall.

Nor is there any will involved in the other person's falling into your life. It just happens. It is simply an outcome of a series of events as you live out your life. The two of you happen to find yourselves working for the same business, or you happen to meet at a bus stop or on a blind date or at a dinner party.

Likewise, if you are married, you were not responsible for choosing to marry. Your decision was beyond choice. For one thing, you were chosen—by the other. For another, your "decision" was no decision at all. You couldn't not marry and still be you. Just as you fell in love, so your decision to marry was beyond your control. It was controlling you; you weren't controlling it. You felt there was a force in you beyond your control pushing you to marry. Love was controlling your life. Obeying the "call" to marry was something you had to do. It was something you couldn't not do.

Hearing the "call" to marry is perhaps the best analogy to hearing the call of God. It has all the earmarks of a call. You are passive in love's power. You feel it in the depths of your soul. You are clearly accessing that "something more" in life. You experience God for perhaps the first time as you find yourself giving God the credit for bringing this other person into your life. "God," you may find yourself saying, "is someone I thank for someone I love."

Then, too, marrying is clearly impossible. It is the last thing you contemplated at this particular moment in your life. Besides, it is clearly impossible that your partner would want to marry you. *How could I possibly be worthy of his or her love?* you find yourself saying. *What have I done to deserve such a blessing in my life?*

Finally, you are transformed. Everything is changed. You have never known such love, joy, peace, patience, kindness, goodness, gentleness, faithfulness and self-control.

The Hidden God Is Revealed

It is, of course, quite possible that these so-called critical events of life will not add up over time and a person will exit life without ever having had an experience of God. Out of thousands of Pharisees, only two are recorded as having had such an experience—Paul and Nicodemus.

We all know people who lead perfectly good lives, have wonderful children, are leaders in the community—and have no experience of the divine dimension at all. Ironically, we also know that in many respects they lead far better lives than their "religious" counterparts. They appear to be more fulfilled and more in touch with who they are. In other words, we may not need God to be happy.

It may be, however, that such people actually have arrived at listening points even though they may not call them such. Possibly God has been present even though they may not use the name *God.* "God," said the poet Edwin Arlington Robinson, "is the name that comes to me when I think and feel how little I have to do with what I am." If the name doesn't come, it could still be God. As another poet wrote, "Truly, thou art a God who hidest thyself" (Is 45:15).

The purpose of this book has been to bring God out of hiding by showing how God was revealed to those who were themselves in hiding, either willfully or not. Moses was in exile. Mary Magdalene was depressed. The prodigal son was a failure. Nicodemus arrived under cover of night.

The hidden God is revealed as the hidden self is drawn out of hiding in response to a call. The hidden self is constantly being prepared by the events of life to hear God's call at various listening points. These preparations add up over time and the inner self is, from time to time, called out, as Jesus called out the hidden Lazarus from his tomb.

When the inner self is called out, salvation comes, at least for the moment, and the fruit of the Spirit in love, joy and peace is experienced. Then, as the inner self slips back into hiding and God recedes from view under the pressure of new events, the calling process starts up again. Subsequent events once more begin to accumulate, and a new listening point is eventually reached.

We call the caller, God. We call the process, grace. We call the naming of God by those who are called, faith. We call what the faithful ones find themselves doing, works. And we call the crises that bring them love, joy and peace, listening points.

Notes

Chapter 2: A Call Is Divine
[1]R. T. Stamm, in *The Interpreter's Bible* (New York: Abingdon, 1953), 10:569.
[2]William Barclay, *The Letters to the Galatians and Ephesians* (Philadelphia: Westminster Press, 1958), p. 56.

Chapter 3: A Call Is Audible
[1]William Barclay, *The Letters to the Corinthians* (Philadelphia: Westminster Press, 1956), p. 44.

Chapter 8: Calls Come in Uncertainty
[1]Chrysostom quoted in William Barclay, *New Testament Words* (London: SCM Press, 1964), p. 145.
[2]Ibid.
[3]William Barclay, *The Acts of the Apostles* (Philadelphia: Westminster Press, 1955), p. 8.

Chapter 10: Calls Come in Emotion
[1]Søren Kierkegaard, *Concluding Unscientific Postscript*, trans. D. Swenson and W. Lowrie (Princeton, N.J.: Princeton University Press, 1944), p. 169.

Chapter 11: Calls Come in Love
[1]*The New International Version Study Bible* (Grand Rapids, Mich.: Zondervan, 1985), p. 365.
[2]Abraham Heschel, quoted in W. A. Johnson's review of *Abraham Heschel's Idea of Revelation*, by Lawrence Perlman, *Christian Century*, April 25, 1990, p. 439.

Chapter 12: Calls Come in Relationships
[1]Aristotle, quoted in William Barclay, *The Letters to Timothy, Titus and Philemon* (Philadelphia: Westminster Press, 1960), p. 311.
[2]Ibid.
[3]Ignatius, *Letter to the Ephesians*, in *The Ante-Nicene Fathers*, ed. A. Roberts and J. Donaldson (Grand Rapids, Mich.: Eerdmans, 1977), 1:49.

Chapter 14: Calls Come in Humility
[1]E. S. Jones, quoted in William Barclay, *The Gospel of Luke* (Philadelphia: Westminster Press, 1956), p. 9.

[2]D. Miller, *The Gospel According to Luke* (Richmond, Va.: John Knox Press, 1959), p. 29.

[3]G. Bertram, "ὑπερηφανος," in *Theological Dictionary of the New Testament*, ed. Gerhard Kittel and Gerhard Friedrich, trans. Geoffrey W. Bromiley (Grand Rapids, Mich.: Eerdmans, 1972), 8:528 n. 29.

[4]Plato *Gorgias* 491e.

[5]K. Rengstorf, "δοῦ λος,"in *Theological Dictionary of the New Testament*, 2:261.

Chapter 17: Calls Come in Discouragement
[1]William Barclay, *The Gospel of Matthew* (Philadelphia: Westminster Press, 1958), 1:336-37
[2]Ibid., pp. 337-38.

Chapter 19: Calls Come in Despair
[1]Paul Tillich, quoted in L. Weatherhead, *The Christian Agnostic* (Nashville: Abingdon, 1965), pp 77-78.

[2]S. Terrien, "Fear," in *The Interpreter's Dictionary of the Bible* (New York: Abingdon, 1962), 2:258

Chapter 20: Calls Come in Frustration
[1]Gerard Manley Hopkins, "The Leaden Echo and the Golden Echo," in *The Poems and Prose of Gerard Manley Hopkins* (Baltimore: Penguin, 1954), pp. 52-54.

Chapter 22: Calls Come in Arrogance
[1]Martin Luther, quoted in E. F. Edinger, *Ego and Archetype* (New York: Putnam, 1972), p. 56.

Chapter 25: Calls Come in Contemplating Scripture
[1]W. Funk, *Word Origins* (New York: Funk, 1950), p. 265.
[2]E. Partridge, *Origins* (New York: Macmillan, 1959), p. 701.
[3]Ibid.

Chapter 28: Calls Come in Dreams
[1]Walter Brueggemann, *Genesis* (Richmond, Va.: John Knox Press, 1982), p. 302.
[2]S. R. Driver, *The Book of Genesis* (London: Methuen, 1954), p. 297. "Some scholars see the struggle as having taken place in a dream" (W. G. Plaut, *The Torah* (New York: Union of American Hebrew Congregations, 1981), p. 221.

Chapter 29: Calls Are Not Heard Because of Greed
[1]C. H. Gordon, "Solomon," in *Encyclopaedia Britannica* (Chicago: University of Chicago Press, 1974), 16:1045.
[2]William Durant, *Our Oriental Heritage* (New York: Simon & Schuster, 1954), p. 308.
[3]Ibid., p. 314.